EASTERN WISDOM IN RISK MANAGEMENT

Reflections of a Chinese Risk Manager

Wen Si

Copyright © 2024 Wen Si

All rights reserved

The characters and events portrayed in this book are fictitious. Any similarity to real persons, living or dead, is coincidental and not intended by the author.

No part of this book may be reproduced, or stored in a retrieval system, or transmitted in any form or by any means, electronic, mechanical, photocopying, recording, or otherwise, without express written permission of the publisher.

ISBN-13: 9798333798602
ISBN-10: 1477123456

Cover design by: Art Painter
Library of Congress Control Number: 2018675309
Printed in the United States of America

To my wife and son, for always loving and supporting me.

CONTENTS

Title Page
Copyright
Dedication
Preface
Understanding Risk — 1
What is Risk Management? — 11
How to Understand the Balance Between Risk and Return? — 26
Why Choose Risk Management as a Personal Career? — 37
From Zero to One in Risk Management — 46
Risk Management Needs Creative Elites — 55
How to Build a Learning-Oriented Risk Management Team — 65
Emotional Intelligence in Risk Management — 73
Risk Management Professionals' Wisdom, Trustworthiness, Benevolence, Courage, and Strictness — 115
About The Author — 155

PREFACE

Since graduating with my master's degree in 2005, I embarked on a career in the financial sector, experiencing various financial forms such as commercial banks, securities firms, trust companies, financial holding groups, and financial asset exchanges. My primary role has been in risk management, witnessing the ups and downs of China's financial industry.

With China's official accession to the World Trade Organization (WTO) in December 2001, the country embarked on a journey of opening its financial sector to the outside world. During this process of opening up, the risk management systems, tools, and methods from mature financial markets were gradually adopted by Chinese financial institutions, giving rise to the new profession of risk manager and attracting an increasing number of outstanding talents to join the ranks of risk managers.

To further develop the private economy, the Chinese government began to promote the opening of finance to domestic private capital in 2013. Regulatory authorities successively granted financial licenses to some domestic private enterprises, including banks, insurance companies, securities firms, trust companies, futures companies, and asset management companies. For a time, the financial industry experienced an unprecedented boom. The newly established financial institutions were in urgent need of a large number of risk managers, and in the labor market, risk managers with certain work experience became highly sought after. It was common for many risk managers to achieve a 50% or even 100% increase in income through job-hopping, marking the most glorious moment for Chinese risk managers.

However, the demand for risk managers in the labor market far exceeded the supply, and the talent gap could only be filled by other financial practitioners lacking in risk management experience or even college graduates. At the same time, learning about risk management became a trend. Against this backdrop, I personally leveraged China's largest social platform, WeChat, to establish the "Dr. CRO" WeChat public account on September 15, 2015. Through this account, I have popularized the concept and ideas of risk management among a wide range of Chinese risk managers and shared experiences in the risk management profession.

Once the bow was drawn, there was no turning back. After nearly a decade of persistence, the "Dr. CRO" WeChat public account has become the most influential and popular WeChat public account in the field of risk management in China, having accumulated the publication of about 500 original risk management articles, of which I personally wrote more than 100 articles. In order to let the world better understand China's risk management and fully comprehend the unique Chinese understanding and approach to risk management, I have selected nine articles from my own and rewritten them in English to compile into this book.

Finally, it needs to be emphasized that due to the absence of financial regulation at the time, coupled with the lack of risk awareness among financial institution management, many private capitals turned the financial institutions they controlled into their own money-making machines and ATMs through improper related transactions and interest transfers. Although most risk managers were dedicated to their work during this period, they were still like 'moths to a flame, and a mantis trying to stop a chariot' – facing an impossible task with limited resources and influence. There is an old Chinese saying: "There is no banquet that does not end, and there is no music that does not stop." Since 2019, the financial industry has been continuously experiencing various financial risk events, the most typical of which are the financial products issued by a large number of private financial institutions to investors, which are essentially Ponzi schemes, causing a large number of investors to lose all their money, with an economic impact comparable to the 2008 U.S. subprime mortgage crisis. Starting in 2020, the Chinese government realized the huge black hole in private finance and decided to take strict regulatory measures against financial institutions, especially private financial institutions. This led to the continuous bursting of financial bubbles and the end of the financial industry's glory. The corresponding unemployment rate also rose continuously. Therefore, this book can also be regarded as a commemoration and memory of the once glorious period of China's risk management!

Wen Si
Shanghai, July 2024

UNDERSTANDING RISK

I have been working in the financial industry for nearly 20 years, dealing with risk on a daily basis, which has led me to constantly ponder the question, "What exactly is risk?" In my spare time, I revisited several classic works in finance, particularly "The Most Important Thing" by Howard Marks, which has deepened and broadened my understanding of risk.

The financial industry operates on risk, and every practitioner is both a bearer and a manager of risk. Therefore, it is essential to truly understand the most fundamental question in finance: "What is risk?" I write this article to share my personal understanding of risk.

1. Biases Towards Risk

Due to my role in risk management, I often contemplate why it is so challenging to advance risk management within Chinese financial institutions, sometimes to the point of difficulty. I once had a conversation with Mr. Zhou, the Chief Risk Officer of a financial institution, who was promoted from the head of a business department. Initially, he believed that his rich business experience and excellent communication skills would allow him to excel in his new role. However, within three months, his initial confidence was almost completely shattered. The root cause was the significant differences, even conflicts, in the understanding of risk among different people within the company.

Generally, the business line, including the business departments and senior executives in charge of business, tends to interpret risk as the potential for achieving returns. In contrast, the risk management line, including the Chief Risk Officer, tends to analyze risk from the perspective of the potential for losses. Due to the different and divergent understandings of risk, communication and discussions about risk are often greatly hindered, often leading to a situation where people talk past each other. Some may ask, "Are these two understandings of risk reasonable?" I personally think these understandings are reasonable, but they are not comprehensive or complete.

1.1 Understanding of Risk from the Business Perspective

The business line is always performance-oriented, striving to achieve results to assert its presence, and these results are often rigidly increasing annually. I recall in 2008, when I served as the assistant general manager of the corporate finance department at a Hong Kong-funded bank's Shanghai branch, our team of four had a performance target of no less than 800 million RMB in loan balances. By 2009, this target had risen to 1.2 billion RMB, with the bank's management setting these targets without considering the worsening global financial crisis. In 2015, I had the opportunity to engage with trust companies and found that domestic trust companies directly set performance targets based on revenue. Typically, a trust business team of four would have an annual revenue target of no less than 30 million RMB, with an annual increase of 10% to 20%. Under such ruthless and short-sighted performance assessments, the business department can only understand, interpret, and perceive risk from the perspective of potential returns, often using slogans like "risk and return match" and "high risk brings high returns." Under the pressure to achieve performance, employees in the business line indeed have no time to seriously consider the true meaning of risk.

1.2 Understanding of Risk from the Risk Management Perspective

It is still necessary to start with the assessment of the risk management line. At present, financial institutions generally use KPIs (Key Performance Indicators) to assess various departments, especially the middle and back offices. For the risk management line, the KPIs mainly focus on the non-performing asset ratio and the proportion of loss assets, such as the non-performing loan ratio (NPL ratio) in banks. From my understanding, many domestic financial institutions, if they have non-performing assets or investment losses, will not only deduct the salaries of the relevant business departments, but also hold the risk management personnel and even the entire risk management department accountable. Such an assessment mechanism is obviously unfair. Some financial institutions' risk management departments have also tried to propose optimization plans to the management, suggesting that if the risk management line maintains due caution and fully performs its duties in the project review process, it can be exempted from joint liability. However, such proposals are usually rejected by the management, on the grounds that the plan is not operable, which is really laughable. Therefore, under such an assessment mechanism, out of self-protection, the risk management line often interprets risk from the perspective of potential losses. At the same time, in order to control potential losses as much as possible, the risk management line will adopt measures such as "reducing credit limits or investment amounts" (professional term is "controlling risk exposure"), "increasing collateral and other security measures" (professional term is "risk mitigation measures"), and the most radical move is to directly veto projects, "better to kill the wrong one than to let go" is also a helpless choice for the risk management line.

For the above two opposing understandings and views, some people take the middle road; they define risk as uncertainty. Uncertainty is indeed one of the most important characteristics of risk, which can include the uncertainty of returns and the uncertainty of losses. However, such an understanding is too simple and crude, and it often misleads people to simply equate risk with uncertainty. If risk is equivalent to uncertainty, then human society does not need to create the term "risk" and can directly use "uncertainty"! The financial industry does not need risk management, just "uncertainty management" will do, and the risk management department can directly change to the "uncertainty management department", and the Chief Risk Officer can directly change to the "Chief Uncertainty Officer", which is really absurd and funny.

2. Personal Understanding Of Risk

Howard Marks in his book "The Most Important Thing" proposed that "risk means the uncertainty of the outcomes that are about to occur, as well as the uncertainty of the probability of adverse outcomes." Some scholars and commentators consider this to be the clearest and most accurate definition of risk they have encountered, but I still believe that such a definition is not comprehensive enough. Therefore, I define risk as "future uncertainty that encompasses the uncertainty of the change process, the uncertainty of the change outcomes, and the unpredictability of losses." In fact, my definition of risk includes three levels: the first level is the uncertainty of the change process, the second level is the uncertainty of the change outcomes, and the third level is the unpredictability of losses. Below is an explanation and discussion in sequence.

2.1 Uncertainty of the Change Process

The uncertainty of the change process is the foundation

of risk. Students majoring in finance at globally renowned universities are required to take the course "Stochastic Processes," a term that perfectly describes the uncertainty of the change process, which is precisely where the charm and magic of finance lie. At this point, some may ask: "What is the root of the uncertainty in the change process in the financial market?" My answer is "Emotion."

South African artist Roger Ballen wrote in the postscript of his book "Theatre of the Absurd": "Human behavior is unreasonable, directionless, and has no ultimate purpose." This aptly describes the absurdity and bizarre nature of human behavior, with the logic behind it being the various emotions of people. The main participants in financial activities are all human beings; investors, operators, policy makers, and market regulators are all people. Since the 1960s, behavioral finance has gradually become an emerging discipline and has been widely recognized. Studying the impact of human emotions on financial activities and financial markets is the cornerstone of this discipline.

Emotion is very important, and the presence of emotions makes the economic and financial operation process full of many variables. At present, "investor sentiment" has been accepted by more and more people. For example, in the commentary of securities analysts on the stock market trend, it is common to hear descriptions of investor sentiment such as "investors are watching the market cautiously." At the same time, depositors also have emotions. For a real example, as mentioned earlier, during the 2008 financial crisis, I was working at a Hong Kong-funded bank and personally experienced the first-ever run on deposits in the bank's history. On the night of the run, Mr. Li Ka-shing, the richest man in Hong Kong, issued a statement supporting the bank's operations and claimed to have increased his deposits in the bank. However, some depositors still went their own way and queued up to withdraw money from the bank.

In addition, policy makers also have emotions, and financial market regulators still have emotions. Taking the stock market crash in China in June and July 2015 as an example, from June 15 to July 8, 2015, in 17 trading days, the Shanghai Composite Index fell from a high of nearly 5,200 points to 3,420 points, a cumulative drop of about 32%, and the small and medium-sized board index and the growth enterprise market index fell even more tragically. During this period, including the People's Bank of China, the China Securities Regulatory Commission, the China Banking Regulatory Commission, the China Insurance Regulatory Commission and other policy makers and market regulators have introduced a variety of measures to save the market. The number and density of rescue measures are unprecedented. I do not judge the correctness of these measures here, I just want to say that because decision-makers are people, they are more or less affected by emotions when introducing these measures.

2.2 Uncertainty of Outcomes

If there is uncertainty in the change process, but the outcome is certain, can this be considered a risk? Definitely not! For a simple example, such as investing in a government bond, although the price of government bonds will fluctuate during their term due to market interest rates and supply and demand, sometimes with significant volatility, the repayment of principal and interest at maturity is certain, so government bonds are generally considered "risk-free assets."

The uncertainty of the outcome is often directly proportional to the number of possible outcomes. For example, tossing a coin has only two outcomes - heads or tails. Although the outcome is uncertain, this type of uncertainty is relatively low, that is, the probability of heads or tails appearing is 50% each; on the contrary, if you toss 10 different coins, the possible number of outcomes is 2 to the power of 10, that is, a total of 1,024 outcomes, and this uncertainty of the outcome is much higher. Given the many complex variables and factors involved in the macroeconomy and financial markets, the uncertainty of the outcome is even higher, often leading to unexpected final results.

Take a recent example: after the Federal Reserve announced a 25 basis point interest rate hike in July 2023, some financial institutions made various predictions about the Federal Reserve cutting interest rates in 2024. The mainstream forecast was that the Federal Reserve would cut rates four times in 2024. However, as of the end of June 2024, the Federal Reserve has remained inactive regarding rate cuts.

Of course, the uncertainty of outcomes also creates a large number of job opportunities in the financial field, the most typical being securities analysts. The main job of securities analysts is to predict the rise and fall of the stock market, colloquially known as "stock market fortune-tellers." Since their predictions are akin to fortune-telling, it's best to take their words with a grain of salt and not act on them blindly. For example, in the first half of 2015, as the Chinese A-share market continued to rise, all analysts were bullish, with some even predicting that the Shanghai Composite Index would break through 10,000 points. At that time, no analyst suggested that the stock market was about to plummet.

In financial risks, the uncertainty of outcomes is always present. Even if some outcomes are predicted correctly, it does not change the inherent uncertainty of outcomes. So-called accurate predictions often rely not on strength and professionalism but on luck and chance.

2.3 Unpredictability of Losses

The unpredictability of losses is the most important feature that distinguishes risk from uncertainty. There are two implications here: first, risk involves losses, and second, these losses are not easy to predict.

Losses refer to the reduction of the initial capital, something all rational investors cannot accept. For a simple example, assume an initial investment of 1 RMB. Even if the loss rate per transaction is only 1%, this means that after 10 consecutive transactions, the principal becomes 0.9 RMB, and after 100 transactions, it's only 0.37 RMB. Therefore, Warren Buffett regards "preserving capital" as the most important investment principle.

Losses are already terrifying, but they are also difficult to predict, which is the most frightening aspect of risk. Any investment with risk has unpredictable losses. No matter how sophisticated the mathematical models or advanced computer systems, they cannot accurately predict losses. The unpredictability of losses includes two dimensions: the unpredictability of the amount of loss and the unpredictability of the probability of loss.

In the financial field, for the convenience of analysis and teaching, it is usually assumed that the distribution of financial asset returns follows a normal distribution. However, the reality is non-normal, especially the tail of the loss distribution is thicker than the normal distribution, hence called "fat tails." Moreover, how fat the tails are and how long the loss tail will drag are very difficult to estimate. In addition, the correlation of returns between different financial assets is also dynamically changing. For example, under normal circumstances, the stock market and the bond market have a seesaw effect, meaning the stock market rises while the bond market falls, and vice versa. However, this pattern is not constant, after all, finance is not a natural science. In 2011, China experienced a stock and bond double kill, with both stock and bond markets falling, completely breaking the seesaw effect. But just three years later, in 2014, China saw a double bull market with both stock and bond markets rising.

Some may ask, why are losses unpredictable? I personally think there are two main reasons: First, the existing data is far from sufficient, especially data involving extreme market conditions is even scarcer. After all, it's not possible to have events like the 2008 global financial crisis and the 2010 European debt crisis every day, right? If that were the case, the financial industry and markets would have been shut down by the government long ago! Second, people's natural aversion to losses often leads to ostrich tactics, estimating losses to be less, which has been proven by behavioral finance. Not only do business departments underestimate potential losses, but risk management departments may also do so under certain circumstances.

In 2012, when I was working in risk management at a securities company, the company's stock was about to be listed on the Chinese A-share market. According to the requirements of the China Securities Regulatory Commission, the company needed to conduct a comprehensive stress test, and the results needed to be reported to the CSRC. After the first round of stress testing by the risk management department, the loss calculated under the worst-case scenario was close to 1 billion RMB. When this result was reported to the Chief Risk Officer, Mr. Li, he was shocked and immediately convened a special meeting on stress testing. At the meeting, Mr. Li emphasized that not only he personally could not accept this test result, but the company's management, shareholders, and even the China Securities Regulatory Commission might not be able to accept it. He demanded an immediate adjustment of various parameters and scenarios to control the maximum loss to within 300 million RMB. I guess similar stories are not isolated cases, and perhaps they are happening every day!

The renowned German sociologist Professor Ulrich Beck published the influential book "Risk Society" as early as 1986, interpreting post-modern society as a society full of risks. Since we live in a society brimming with risks, instead of evading, it is better to face it actively and take the initiative to understand and comprehend risks. Of course, our exploration of risk is like the exploration of the vast universe, which is endless, and our cognition of risk is always on the journey.

WHAT IS RISK MANAGEMENT?

In April 2016, after an eighteen-year absence, I had the opportunity to revisit my alma mater, Huzhou High School, and met my math teacher, Mr. Feng, whom I hadn't seen for nearly two decades. When Mr. Feng asked me what I was currently doing for a living, I replied, "I am employed in the risk management division of a financial institution." He then inquired, "What is risk management?" I was momentarily at a loss for words, as I hadn't fully considered what risk management entailed, nor had I thought about how to describe it in layman's terms to someone outside the financial sector. Seeing my hesitation, Mr. Feng remarked, "Risk management must surely be a highly specialized and somewhat enigmatic profession!" After much contemplation, I decided to pen this article in an attempt to demystify the enigmatic "black box" of risk management.

In the "Biographies of Merchants" from the Records of the Grand Historian, it is written: "The world is bustling, all for the sake of profit; the world is noisy, all for the pursuit of gain." These sixteen characters succinctly capture the profit-seeking nature of capital. Financial institutions, as stewards of substantial capital, naturally aim to preserve and increase the value of capital as their primary means of survival. However, in the pursuit of capital gains, they must also bear risks.

The financial industry itself is an industry that operates and manages risks. In short, risk management is the management of risks, which I personally summarize as the "identification, assessment, monitoring, and control" of risks. Let's discuss this in detail.

1. The "Identification" Of Risk

In the Apollo Temple in Bassae, Greece, there is one of the most famous aphorisms: "Know thyself." Similarly, since financial institutions face various risks at all times, the primary task of risk management is to recognize and identify these risks. These risks mainly include market risk, credit risk, liquidity risk, and operational risk.

1.1 Market Risk

Investors in stocks are most concerned about stock price declines, which can lead to investment losses; depositors worry about the People's Bank of China lowering deposit interest rates, while home loan borrowers worry about the People's Bank of China raising loan interest rates. Changes in interest rates affect the interest income of depositors and the interest expenses of home loan borrowers; buyers of imported goods worry about the depreciation of the renminbi, which increases their expenses; white-collar workers who drive to work worry about rising oil prices, which increase the cost of travel. These examples, where stock price fluctuations, interest rate adjustments, exchange rate changes, and commodity price movements lead to reduced income, losses, or increased expenses, are known as "market risk" because these risks directly come from the market.

To understand the nature of market risk, it is important to recognize its main causes: the first is the psychology of market participants, including greed, envy, arrogance, gullibility, herd mentality, and fear, which are often manifested in the financial market as blind trust in well-known analysts, envy of others' investment gains, overconfidence and blind optimism from brief successes, greed in chasing rising prices, and fear in falling markets. The second cause is cycles, including economic and industry cycles. The reasons for these cycles are mainly twofold: one is the market's self-regulation, the invisible hand, which led to the severe consequences of the 1997 Asian financial crisis and the 2008 global financial tsunami; the other is government intervention, the visible hand, such as the relaxation and even cancellation of real estate purchase restrictions and loan policies in many cities in China since the beginning of 2024. The real estate industry's prosperity is expected to turn upward. At the same time, based on my personal observations, minor market fluctuations often stem from psychology, while major fluctuations usually originate from cycles.

1.2 Credit Risk

I remember when I was in elementary school, there was a classmate who often borrowed money from other students to buy snacks and promised to pay back in a short time. However, when asked to repay, he would often shrug his shoulders, indicating he had no money to repay, or sometimes he would simply say he had never borrowed. Borrowing money without intending to repay, failing to fulfill promises, is known as "credit risk," which is the risk caused by the other party's lack of creditworthiness. The roots of credit risk include the subjective intention not to repay or fulfill obligations and the objective inability to repay or fulfill obligations. Commercial banks, trust companies, and other financial institutions face the greatest risk in their operations, which is credit risk. Credit risk affects the sensitive nerves of many people in these financial institutions and is closely linked to personal income.

Since 2012, China's internet finance industry has seen rapid development, and P2P online lending has quickly become popular among the general public. However, various extreme events such as the bankruptcy of P2P platforms and the flight of their bosses have become increasingly intense. On October 13, 2016, the Chinese government issued the "Special Rectification Plan for Internet Finance Risks," which clearly targeted P2P online lending as one of the key issues to be rectified because the credit risk involved in P2P online lending is too great. At the end of 2014, I was invited to give a speech on internet finance at a municipal party school in a prefecture-level city in eastern China. After the speech, some government officials asked me whether they could buy some high-yield P2P products. My answer was straightforward: "Do not touch them." The seemingly attractive high returns hide the possibility of a total loss, and there is no need to risk one's hard-earned money with such high risks. Traditional commercial bank deposits are the safest way.

1.3 Liquidity Risk

There is a saying in the financial market: "Cash is king." Capital is the lifeblood of economic operations and also the lifeline of a company or financial institution. When a company or financial institution cannot raise funds when needed, or when they need to sell assets but face a situation where there are no buyers, this is known as "liquidity risk." Let's consider two real-life examples.

The first example: In 2011, many enterprises in Wenzhou, China, faced bankruptcy due to banks stopping loan disbursements. A colleague of mine happened to be from Wenzhou, and his parents owned their own business. He told me that in 2011, some banks would verbally promise to issue a new loan to enterprises after the repayment of the existing loan. However, when the enterprises managed to gather funds to repay the loans, the banks would then stop issuing subsequent loans for various reasons, leading to the breaking of the capital chain for many Wenzhou enterprises, ultimately resulting in bankruptcy or the owners fleeing.

The second example: Compared to mature capital markets, the A-share market in China has a unique trading rule, which is the daily limit up and limit down rule. When there is a need to sell a large amount of a certain stock in the market, the excessive sell orders may cause the stock price to hit the lower limit, making it difficult to sell more stocks. If the lower limit is opened, it's somewhat better; if it remains firmly closed, one can only wait until the next trading day to sell. If one is unfortunately heavily invested in a stock that has hit the lower limit for several consecutive days, it is truly tragic because buyers seem to have vanished!

1.4 Operational Risk

Financial activities are carried out through people and information technology. The French thinker of the Renaissance, Michel de Montaigne, once pointed out: "Man is a constantly changing creature, a purely potential existence, and does not necessarily lead to what was once considered true, good, and beautiful." Therefore, people can make mistakes and do bad things, which is an operational risk. When I just graduated from my master's degree, I worked in a branch of a joint-stock bank and personally heard about the bank's tellers and account managers embezzling funds to gamble in Macau and buy luxury goods, which is an astonishing act. Therefore, financial institutions must always be vigilant about the actions of people.

The advent of computers and the development of information technology have greatly facilitated people's life and work, but they often catch people off guard, such as the "Everbright Securities 'Fat Finger' incident" that shocked China and the world on August 16, 2013. The cause of this incident was a defect in the company's internal trading system, which is a typical operational risk event. The incident finally ended with Everbright Securities being punished and the parties involved being held accountable. As humanity is entering the era of general artificial intelligence, with the rapid development of artificial intelligence, there are more and more artificial intelligence trading programs participating in the capital market. How to prevent operational risk events caused by artificial intelligence has been on the agenda of financial institutions.

2. The "Assessment" Of Risk

After financial institutions have recognized and identified risks, the next step is to assess and judge these risks. The methods of risk assessment are qualitative and quantitative, and the judgment of risks needs to be combined with the institution's own preferences and tolerance levels.

2.1 Qualitative and Quantitative Assessment of Risks

Qualitative assessment of risks relies on the accumulation of experience, which is similar to driving a car. Why do experienced drivers have more driving experience than novices? This is because experienced drivers have been through various road conditions and have seen or even encountered various accidents. In 2006, I was working in the Shanghai branch of a foreign bank in corporate lending. At that time, we were quite optimistic about a Taiwan-funded enterprise in Suzhou, China, applying for a loan. When the loan application was reported to the head office's risk management department, the risk controller who reviewed this loan had been working in the financial industry for more than ten years and had visited hundreds of companies of all sizes on site. After carefully reading the submitted materials, he felt that the company's business development was too fast and seemed unreliable, and finally rejected the loan. Two years later, the company eventually went bankrupt due to a broken capital chain, and many commercial banks were involved, while the bank where I worked successfully avoided this time bomb. Therefore, from this perspective, risk management work is more suitable for people with rich experience and life experience.

Risks also need to be quantitatively measured to determine whether the risk is large or small, high or low. Quantitative measurement of risks is similar to blood tests performed by hospitals on patients, including more than ten quantitative indicators such as white blood cells, platelets, and hemoglobin. Once when I went to the hospital for treatment, I joked with the doctor, saying, "In the future, patients who feel unwell can go directly to the hospital for a blood test, and then the computer can directly give a conclusion based on the blood test results, whether they are sick and what disease they have, so the doctor will be relieved!" The doctor's response was very serious and professional, saying, "The results of the blood test are for reference and must be corroborated with other evidence, and cannot simply replace the doctor's clinical judgment." Similarly, the quantitative measurement of risks is to provide a reference for the final decision, and the decision must still be made by people. At the same time, the quantitative measurement of risks needs to rely on strong information technology means. An important part of risk management is the development of risk management systems. Financial institutions generally do not develop on their own because they do not have this level and do not have so many talents, and they need to cooperate with domestic and foreign professional risk management system developers.

Risks sometimes have contagiousness like viruses, mainly including the transmission within the same type of risk and the infection between different types of risks, forming a domino effect. The measurement of this contagiousness requires the use of "correlation" in statistics. Let's give two examples of transmission within the same risk: the sharp drop in China's A-share market from June to July 2015, which led to violent fluctuations in the stock markets of the Asia-Pacific region, including Hong Kong, Japan, and the United States; on August 11, 2015, the People's Bank of China adjusted the pricing rules for the central parity rate of the renminbi, which not only caused a short-term depreciation of the renminbi against the US dollar but also caused a competitive depreciation of the currencies of emerging market countries against the US dollar. Let's give an example of infection between different types of risks: the "Fat Finger Incident" of Everbright Securities on August 16, 2013. Although this incident was an operational risk event within a financial institution, it led to violent fluctuations in the A-share market in the short term and increased market risk.

2.2 Risk Preference and Risk Tolerance

After the risk assessment is completed, it needs to be compared with the financial institution's own risk preference and risk tolerance, so as to finally make a judgment and decision on whether to take risks or to avoid risks.

The risk preference of a financial institution, in a nutshell, is to choose what kind of customers, what kind of business, and what kind of products to develop, which is very similar to the blind date between men and women, and there are also qualitative and quantitative differences. For example, some single women born after 1995, when asking for help to introduce a partner, usually have specific requirements such as the man's appearance should be high, his character should be good, and his education should not be lower than a master's degree, which are qualitative preference indicators; the man's height should be between 1.75 meters and 1.85 meters, the annual pre-tax income should not be lower than 500,000 yuan, and the age should be between 30 and 35 years old, which are quantitative preference indicators. The design of financial institutions' risk preferences should be reasonable and not too high. If a rural bank requires loan customers to be among the top 500 companies in the world, it is estimated that the leaders and employees of this bank will have to go to the northwest wind, but it should not be designed too low, otherwise it will bear too much, too high, and excessive risks.

Risk tolerance refers to the extent of loss that a financial institution can withstand. The size of risk tolerance is closely related to the capital strength of the financial institution. China's state-owned large commercial banks such as ICBC, CCB, ABC, and BOC have strong capital strength, so their tolerance for various risks is relatively high, and a few hundred million yuan of non-performing loans are just a drop in the bucket for these banks; in contrast, rural banks or rural credit cooperatives have weaker capital strength, so their tolerance for risk is relatively low, and a non-performing loan of 100 million yuan may be fatal to these banks.

Of course, the design of risk preference and risk tolerance is a headache in risk management, which needs to be considered comprehensively according to the financial institution's business strategy, competitive environment, financial budget, performance targets, and other factors, and is often the focus of the game between the risk management department and the business department.

3. The "Monitoring" Of Risk

The ancient Greek philosopher Heraclitus famously said, "One cannot step into the same river twice," revealing that change is an eternal characteristic of all things. Risk itself is a form of future uncertainty, so change is an essential feature of risk. Every day, the capital market fluctuates like the tides of the Qiantang River. A macroeconomic downturn can make previously high-quality borrowers lose their debt repayment capacity, and policy changes can turn once highly profitable investments into total losses. Therefore, financial institutions need to dynamically track and monitor risks, which usually include three aspects of work: collecting the latest information of existing customers, tracking the dynamic changes of the capital market, and participating in the daily supervision of industrial projects.

3.1 Collecting the Latest Information of Existing Customers

In 2015, I worked at a trust company where the risk management department established a special team responsible for collecting the latest information on existing financing customers and invested enterprises. From the moment they started work at 8:30 in the morning, they used the internet and specialized financial databases to collect as much up-to-date information on these customers as possible, and formed written reports. These reports were submitted to the company's management and uploaded to the company's office system for reference by all employees. The report often exceeded 100 pages. At a company office meeting, the president jokingly said that this team was the intelligence center of the entire company.

In addition to collecting information from the internet, financial institutions regularly and irregularly inspect physical enterprises to timely grasp key information such as whether the factory is in operation, whether the operation is stable, whether sales are good, and whether capital is returned in time.

3.2 Tracking the Dynamic Changes of the Capital Market

The father of global investment, John Templeton, once said, "The market always appears in despair, grows in hesitation, matures in longing, and ends in madness." For securities companies, fund companies, asset management companies, and other financial institutions that actively participate in the capital market, a key task of risk management is to dynamically track investments in the capital market and factors affecting investment value in real time.

The "Shanghai Securities News" published an article on October 14, 2016, titled "Controlling 1.27 Trillion Market Value, A-Share Capital Creates System Trajectory." The reporter sorted out the various "systems" in China's capital market, listing a total of 20 systems, including Bao Neng, Ming Tian, and Zhong Zhi, each controlling many domestic listed companies. Behind each aggressively expanding capital system, there is often a sensitive and taut capital chain, and once a link in the chain has a problem, it can lead to the collapse of the entire capital and industrial chain in a short period of time. The "De Long System" at the beginning of the 21st century had the brilliant past but eventually perished, which is a painful lesson. In April 2004, I was studying for my master's degree and happened to be interning at a consulting company when the "De Long System" had an accident. The stock prices of its three stocks, "Xinjiang Tunhe," "He Jin Shares," and "Xiang Torch," had several consecutive daily limit declines. At that time, I had an impulse to use a few months of internship income to bottom out these stocks, but in the end, I still felt that the risk was too high and did not try it. Fortunately, I escaped a disaster.

3.3 Participating in the Daily Management of Industrial Projects

The core of finance is to serve the real economy. Since 2016, more and more financial institutions have started to take the road of combining industry with finance, and they often send employees to participate in the daily operation and management of specific invested industrial projects, in order to dynamically and comprehensively grasp the changes in project risks.

In August 2016, I went to a trust company listed on the A-share market to participate in an exchange of risk management experience and learned that this trust company was doing well in the combination of industry and finance. The main model is to invest in some medium-sized real estate companies in China through the issuance of trust products to achieve "risk sharing and benefit sharing." In this regard, the company recruited employees from well-known real estate developers and established an investment management department. Financial personnel were stationed on the spot in the invested real estate projects to grasp the information of each fund expenditure and external transfer, and professional cost engineers were also assigned to strictly track the project progress and cost.

4. The "Control" Of Risk

If the operation of financial institutions is likened to flying a kite, then the control of risk is like the kite flyer firmly holding the string connecting the kite. No matter how high or far the kite flies, this string must never loosen or break. The domestic financial industry often equates risk control with risk management, which highlights the important role of risk control to a certain extent. In fact, risk control is only an integral part of risk management. To express it in mathematical terms, risk management is the "whole set," and risk control is the "true subset." There are many methods and means of risk control, including risk diversification, profit-taking, and stop-loss.

4.1 Risk Diversification

Investors often say, "Don't put all your eggs in one basket," which reveals the essence of risk diversification. Risk diversification is ubiquitous in financial activities.

Suppose a commercial bank only grants loans to one company, and if this company unfortunately goes bankrupt, then the bank is also likely to go bankrupt. Therefore, banks grant loans to different corporate customers and individual customers, after all, it is not likely that all corporate and individual customers will go bankrupt at the same time.

In the fund products issued by fund companies, fund managers do not invest all the funds in one stock, but diversify investments, such as allocating some funds to blue-chip stocks and the remaining funds to the Science and Technology Innovation Board and the Growth Enterprise Market stocks; with the acceleration of the interconnection process between the Chinese A-share stock market and overseas markets such as the Hong Kong stock market, allocating some funds to overseas capital markets has become a trend. After all, the market often appears "the east is not bright, the west is bright," and diversifying investments is conducive to smoothing returns and controlling risks.

4.2. Profit-Taking and Stop-Loss

Investment master Warren Buffett once said, "Investors almost don't need to do anything right, just avoid major mistakes," and to avoid major mistakes, you need to use "profit-taking and stop-loss." Profit-taking is "locking in profits," and stop-loss is "admitting defeat and exiting."

Let's first talk about profit-taking. In May 2015, when I was discussing the stock market with Mr. Tan, the deputy general manager of a trust company, I analyzed that in a bull market driven by capital leverage, due to the excessively fast rise in stock indexes, it is necessary to be particularly vigilant about the cliff-like decline of the stock market in the future. In this regard, I proposed two risk control suggestions: one is to use stock index futures for hedging the stock position to lock in profits. At that time, I also researched some well-known private equity funds and asset management companies, and these financial institutions have mostly taken this operation in a forward-looking manner; the second is to set a profit-taking liquidation line, once the stock price falls to a psychological price, resolutely liquidate and exit, to protect the fruits of victory, and not to harbor illusions about possible rebounds in the future.

Then let's talk about stop-loss. Another investment master Howard Marks once said, "Avoiding losses is more important than great success." Therefore, whether it is in stock investment or in higher-risk futures trading, a stop-loss line will be set; for example, if the initial net value of a stock-type fund is 1 yuan per share, and the set stop-loss line is 0.9 yuan per share, then when the stock price falls and the fund net value touches 0.9 yuan per share, the fund manager will sell stocks to control the loss.

Investment business needs stop-loss, and banks also have a mechanism similar to stop-loss when carrying out loan business, such as when the bank finds that the borrower is unable to repay the loan, it will decisively adopt measures such as freezing account funds, disposing of collateral and pledge, and recovering from the guarantor, thereby controlling the risk.

Some people may ask, what are the consequences of not having a stop-loss mechanism? Here is a real-life example. The Shanghai Composite Index of China's A-shares reached the highest of 6124.04 points on October 16, 2007, and in 2008, the "Olympic year," it was in a downward channel. At that time, a large domestic securities company did not take stop-loss measures, resulting in huge losses in the company's proprietary securities investment, which shattered the dream of going public in the A-share market in 2009. It was not until 2015 that the company finally realized its dream in the A-share market. Since 2009, a key task of this company's risk management has been to establish and improve a stop-loss mechanism for proprietary securities investment to prevent the tragedy from happening again.

Finally, after completing this article, I sent the article to my high school math teacher, Mr. Feng. A few days later, Mr. Feng mentioned in his reply to me: "I took the time to read this article carefully and finally understood risk management, and also found that risk management is indeed quite advanced and sophisticated!"

HOW TO UNDERSTAND THE BALANCE BETWEEN RISK AND RETURN?

Working in the financial industry for a long time, one often hears the phrase: "Finance is all about seeking a balance between risk and return." The first time I heard this, it reminded me of the balance scale we used in junior high physics class, where the left side of the scale is usually for the object to be weighed, and the right side is for the weights. So, I initially fantasized that in the financial system, there might also be such a tangible or intangible balance scale, with risk on the left and return on the right, and then weigh them. If the two sides are not balanced, either add or subtract some risk to the left or some return to the right. Obviously, such a thought is quite naive and unrealistic. In the field of finance, taking risks does not necessarily guarantee returns, and achieving returns is far from as simple as desiring them.

So, let's talk about how to understand the balance between risk and return. The article unfolds in three aspects: first, discussing the complexity of measuring risk; second, analyzing the consistency between subjective risk and expected return rate before the event (for example, when making investment decisions); and third, analyzing the new balance formed between subjective risk and actual return rate after the event (for example, when the investment ends).

1. The Complexity Of Measuring Risk

The concept of "balance between risk and return" originated from the Capital Asset Pricing Model (CAPM) proposed by William Sharpe in the 1960s and the Efficient Market Hypothesis proposed by Eugene Fama in the 1970s.

Here, I will not comment on the correctness of the Capital Asset Pricing Model and the Efficient Market Hypothesis. The phrase "balance between risk and return" itself requires a prerequisite, that is, both risk and return need to be quantifiable. Things that cannot be quantified are difficult to balance. Returns can be measured in numbers, usually in percentages, and the standard of measurement is unified, which is acceptable to everyone. However, compared to returns, quantifying risk is not an easy task. Risk is invisible and intangible, a bit like a saying in "The Classic of the Virtue of the Tao" (by the ancient philosopher Lao Zi) - "Mysterious and profound, the gateway to all secrets." Therefore, since the 1950s, a group of European and American economists have tried to use mathematical statistics to quantify risk, including using volatility (standard deviation), beta value, and Value at Risk (VaR) and other indicators to measure risk. Some even rely on rocket scientists to complete the risk measurement.

However, finance is not physics, and the purity of theory often encounters the embarrassment of reality, especially in Chinese financial institutions that rely more on qualitative analysis and experience judgment, where the work of risk quantification is even more difficult. From 2010 to 2014, I was engaged in risk management work in a Chinese securities company. An important work content and performance assessment indicator was to improve the quantification level of the company's risk management. At that time, I was full of beautiful expectations and infinite longing for risk quantification. However, in a company's internal training on how to quantify risk, some company leaders and business department heads questioned the rationality and effectiveness of using risk value and other indicators to quantify risk, which made me sweat. After the training, the company's CEO, Mr. Jin, patted me on the shoulder and comforted me, saying, "The work of risk quantification is quite important, but it needs to be more in line with the actual situation of China's capital market and the company's actual situation, and to be more grounded." Although he said so, when I left the securities company in 2014, the work of risk quantification was still in a very primitive stage.

2. Pre-Event: Consistency Between Subjective Risk And Expected Rate Of Return

My first level of understanding of "risk and return balance" is before the event, such as when making investment decisions, striving to maintain the consistency between subjective risk and expected rate of return. Since the expected rate of return is a compensation for taking risks, a subjectively low risk should match a lower expected rate of return, and a subjectively high risk should match a higher expected rate of return. This is also the inherent meaning of financial theories such as the Capital Asset Pricing Model and the Efficient Market Hypothesis, after all, people are rational animals, and financial decision-makers are even more rational and professional. Therefore, each financial decision is actually a process of measuring whether subjective risk and expected rate of return are matched.

2.1 Subjective Judgment of Risk

Since financial decisions depend on human completion, the judgment of risk also depends on human subjective judgment. Note that this subjective risk judgment includes both internal assessments within financial institutions and external third-party assessments.

First, let's talk about how institutions internally judge risk.

The risk judgment here is definitely not just the judgment of the risk manager, nor just the judgment of the risk management department, nor just the judgment of the Chief Risk Officer, after all, different people have different judgments of risk. A hundred people read "Dream of the Red Chamber" and there are a hundred Lin Dais, a thousand people see "Hamlet" and there are a thousand different Hamlets. In a standardized financial institution, the judgment of risk is a collective decision-making process, usually a detailed risk assessment report is issued by the risk management department and submitted to the credit approval committee (banks), investment decision committee (non-bank financial institutions) and other deliberative bodies for the final collective decision. Such a committee is usually composed of 7-9 members and adopts a majority agreement rule. Experimental psychology has provided a lot of evidence that individual judgments of things are often less dependent on rational assessment, and sometimes are even based on some incredible ideas. Therefore, compared to individual decision-making, collective decision-making can make full use of individual expertise and information, effectively prevent individual cognitive biases and psychological emotions on the basis of brainstorming.

I can give a real example. In May 2015, when I was working in a trust company, the business department submitted a financial management product plan mainly aimed at investing in the directed issuance of Chinese A-shares. Considering that the price of directed issuance stocks will have a certain discount rate, the risk management department believes that the risk of this product is relatively low, and the company's CEO also expressed recognition and support. However, the final vote of the company's investment decision committee was 5 votes against and 2 votes in favor, and the plan was rejected. At that time, the Shanghai Composite Index had already exceeded 4,000 points, and most of the committee members believed that the valuation of the A-share market was too high, and the investment strategy of investing in directed issuance stocks at this time would face a higher risk. The final facts also confirmed the rationality of the collective decision of the investment decision committee.

Next, let's talk about third-party risk assessment.

Generally speaking, external third-party risk assessment often refers to the external credit rating of credit rating agencies. Standard & Poor's, Moody's, and Fitch almost monopolize the global financial market's credit rating. In China, there are only less than 10 rating companies that carry out credit rating business, such as Dagong Global Credit Rating Co., Ltd. (referred to as "Dagong Global"), China Chengxin International Credit Rating Co., Ltd. (referred to as "China Chengxin International"), United Credit Ratings Co., Ltd. (referred to as "United Ratings"), Shanghai New Century Credit Rating Investment Services Co., Ltd. (referred to as "New Century Ratings"), etc.

In 2016, when I was introducing external credit risk ratings to students at Renmin University of China, a student asked a very good question: "Since there are external credit ratings, why do financial institutions still need internal risk judgment? Isn't it just a matter of taking it directly?" In response to this question, I gave three reasons. The first reason is that the ratings of external rating agencies are based on the agency's own professionalism and standards, which can be used for reference, but cannot simply replace the internal judgment of financial institutions. There are often discrepancies or even contradictions between the internal judgment of financial institutions and external ratings. The second reason is that the subjects covered by external ratings are too few, usually for companies that need to issue bonds, but the counterparties of financial institutions are much broader. The third reason is that external ratings focus on the assessment of credit risk, which is not applicable to investment products at all.

2.2 Expected Rate of Return

In the financial field, when it comes to the rate of return, there are two related but different rates of return - expected rate of return and actual rate of return. The actual rate of return generally obeys a certain statistical distribution (discrete or continuous distribution), and often presents a distribution that is similar to normal but not entirely normal. To simplify the analysis, people will use the expected rate of return beforehand. The expected rate of return here is defined in a statistical way, usually equivalent to the expected value (also known as the "mean") in statistics. For example, if a financial product has four possible actual rates of return upon maturity, 0%, 2%, 4%, and 6%, and each rate of return has the same probability of occurrence (i.e., 25%), the expected rate of return for the product is 3%. Please note here, do not confuse the expected rate of return with the actual rate of return. The expected rate of return is before the event, and the actual rate of return is after the event. The actual rate of return may or may not be equal to the expected rate of return, and it is often not equal to the expected rate of return. However, according to my personal observation, the confusion between the expected rate of return and the actual rate of return is not only common among newcomers in the financial workplace but also often occurs among senior financial professionals.

Within large financial institutions, a financial product map is compiled according to the expected rate of return. Generally speaking, the expected rate of return for equity products is higher than that for debt products (such as bonds, bank loans, etc.), and the expected rate of return for debt products is higher than that for monetary products (such as money market funds, bank deposits, etc.). For debt products, the expected rate of return for corporate debtors is higher than that for government debtors, the expected rate of return for private enterprise debtors is higher than that for state-owned enterprise debtors, and the expected rate of return for non-bank financial institution issuers (such as trusts, wealth management products) is often higher than that for commercial bank issuers (such as bank wealth management products), and so on.

3. Post-Event: A New Balance Between Subjective Risk And Actual Rate Of Return

As mentioned earlier, the subjective risk before the event is matched with the expected rate of return. When the expected rate of return is transformed into the actual rate of return after the event, a new balance is formed between subjective risk and actual rate of return, which includes two levels of meaning. The first level of meaning is the four normal balances formed under normal financial market conditions: the balance between subjective low risk and actual low rate of return, the balance between subjective low risk and actual low loss rate, the balance between subjective high risk and actual high rate of return, and the balance between subjective high risk and actual high loss rate. The second level of meaning is the mutational, abnormal balance under abnormal financial market conditions, mainly including two categories: one is the balance between subjective low risk and actual high rate of return, and the other is the balance between subjective low risk and actual high loss rate. This is my second level of understanding of "risk and return balance," and I will now analyze the abnormal balance of risk and return in detail.

3.1 Subjective Low Risk Achieving Actual High Rate of Return

Generally speaking, it is a normal state for subjectively considered low risk to ultimately achieve a stable low return.

However, under specific conditions, high returns can be obtained. Such investment opportunities are what all financial institutions and investors dream of and compete for. Of course, such opportunities are not only few but also very scarce, and they often appear only when the market is distorted. Here are two examples.

The first example occurred during the 2008 global financial crisis when U.S. Treasury bonds became very popular. During the financial crisis, almost all investors chose to avoid risk at the same time in terms of risk preference, and they all chose "Flight to Quality" in investment decisions, which led to funds pouring into safe and highly liquid U.S. Treasury bonds. In the fourth quarter of 2008, when the financial crisis reached its peak, the maximum decline in the yield to maturity (YTM) of 20-year and 30-year U.S. Treasury bonds reached 180 basis points. If calculated conservatively with a duration of 10 times, the increase in the price of U.S. Treasury bonds would be 18%. In just a few months, U.S. Treasury bonds had such an astonishing increase, which can be said to be a high-yield investment.

The second example involves a classmate of mine who is very keen on investing in Chinese A-shares. However, in December 2012, when the Shanghai Composite Index was around 2000 points and even dropped to a low of 1950, his stock investment performance was very poor, with losses exceeding 40%. He asked me for my views on the future of the stock market, and I replied, "From the perspective of the relationship between price and value, the intrinsic value of A-shares at 2000 points is already significantly higher than the market price, and stock investment is in a low-risk area. Warren Buffett has a famous saying: 'Be greedy when others are fearful, and be fearful when others are greedy!' As long as you have some patience, the future investment returns will be quite good!" After careful analysis, my classmate followed my advice, not only did he not cut his losses at that time, but instead, he took the opportunity to increase his holdings. A year and a half later (in June 2014), the Chinese A-shares entered a bull market that lasted for a year, and my classmate's stock investment also successfully turned losses into profits, which was also worthy of his hard-earned money.

3.2 Subjective Low Risk Turning into Actual High Loss Rate

When a subjectively low risk turns into an actual huge loss, this is the black swan event in the financial field, which requires investors to be vigilant and actively guard against it. Nassim Nicholas Taleb's book "The Black Swan" mentions that "The existence of black swans implies unpredictable major rare events. Humans always over-rely on experience, and do not know that the appearance of a black swan is enough to subvert everything." The black swan event in the financial field is very similar to an upset in a sports game. For example, on October 6, 2016, in the World Cup qualifier, the Chinese national football team played against the Syrian national football team. Before the game, almost everyone thought that the Chinese national football team had a great chance of winning the game, but the result was a 0-1 defeat. Regarding the situation where subjective low risk ultimately leads to actual high losses, I will give two specific examples.

The first example occurred before the 2008 global financial crisis, where the senior tranches of collateralized debt obligations (CDOs) were often given the highest AAA credit ratings by external rating agencies. Such ratings are the same as the ratings for U.S. Treasury bonds, but the yield levels are much higher than U.S. Treasury bonds, leading many financial institutions to compete for purchase. For a long period of time, there were no default events in the senior tranches of collateralized debt obligations, so almost all financial institutions regarded the senior tranches of CDOs as the holy grail of risk-free investment before the crisis, and a hot-hand effect was formed among investors. The hot-hand effect refers to the process in a basketball game where if a player makes consecutive shots, other players will believe that he has a "hot hand," and will choose him to shoot again next time, thinking that his probability of making a shot is 100%, but in fact, the probability of the player making the next shot is still 50%. The final result was that the senior tranches of CDOs became a nightmare for various financial institutions, which was vividly described in the 2016 Hollywood movie "The Big Short."

The second example is the collapse of the rigid payment belief in China's domestic bond market. Before 2013, there was a belief in the bond market that bonds would not default. Under such a belief, there was no difference in actual risk between AAA-rated bonds and AA-rated bonds, but the coupon rates of the bonds were far apart. The coupon rate of AA-rated bonds is generally 300 to 400 basis points higher than that of AAA-rated bonds. At that time, many institutional investors in China used repurchase transactions to leverage, buying a large number of low-rated bonds, eating the interest rate spread between the bond coupon rate and the repurchase rate. This kind of transaction is called a "low-risk bond spread trading strategy." However, the American writer Mark Twain has a famous saying: "People are not burdened by what they don't know, but by what they believe without doubt." When this deeply believed low-risk investment strategy encountered a bond default event, it got into big trouble. Since the default of Chaori bond in 2014, which opened the precedent for bond defaults in China, the default of the bond market has shown an explosive growth. With the normalization of bond defaults, the possibility of huge losses from the low-risk bond spread trading strategy has been increasing, and the good old days of making a sure profit have become a thing of the past.

The phrase "risk and return balance" seems simple, but it is profound and rich in connotation, which requires every financial person to think carefully and weigh it from time to time.

WHY CHOOSE RISK MANAGEMENT AS A PERSONAL CAREER?

One day in September 2016, I had lunch with my former boss, Ms. Cheung, the head of a foreign bank's Shanghai branch. It had been a long time since I left the bank in early 2010, and our reunion was particularly cordial. During our casual conversation, Ms. Cheung suddenly asked me, "At that time, you were a backbone of the branch's business, and you did very well in corporate credit business. If you hadn't chosen to leave, you would have had the opportunity to be promoted to deputy head of the branch now. Do you regret leaving the front-line business position to engage in the risk management work in the middle and back office?" I answered without hesitation, " Ms. Cheung, to be honest, there have been some things in my personal learning and work that I regret. But choosing to engage in risk management work is what I think is the most correct thing in my life!"

Ms. Cheung was very curious and asked for the reasons. I pondered for a moment and replied, "Engaging in risk management work brings three unique values: exposure to a broader range of business, working with excellent colleagues, and meeting outstanding leaders!" Ms. Cheung smiled slightly and said, "That's quite good! Congratulations!" After lunch, I hurried home and wrote this article, trying to fully elaborate and reasonably prove the three major values of choosing risk management as a personal career.

1. Value One: Exposure To A Broader Range Of Business

In April 2016, Phil Knight, the founder of Nike, published his autobiography "Shoe Dog," which he wrote himself. The sentence I appreciate the most in the book is "Life is growth, you grow or you die." This sentence is very applicable to the financial workplace. After all, the financial industry is an industry with "talent" as its core competitiveness, and financial work is a very professional job. The core competitiveness of financial talents in the workplace is professional ability.

I often make such a metaphor: A person's career is like a castle, and individuals need to think about how to widen the moat of this castle. In the financial industry, exposure to and learning of more business, especially innovative business and cutting-edge products, is often the best way to widen the moat of personal careers. Some people may say, "All roads lead to Rome," and there are various ways to learn about business and familiarize with products, such as taking financial certificate exams, participating in product business training, and reading professional books and articles. However, "knowledge from books is always shallow, only through practice can one truly understand," and risk management work provides the most convenient and effective "practice" path.

Since the COSO (Committee of Sponsoring Organizations of the Treadway Commission) published "Enterprise Risk Management - Integrated Framework" in the United States in 2004, more and more financial institutions have begun to practice the concept and culture of comprehensive risk management. All internal business of a financial institution, especially innovative and complex products, requires the participation of the risk management team in all aspects and the entire process. At the same time, the most critical, core, and valuable content in business and products is the risk management system and risk control plan. Risk management is not only the focus of external regulatory agencies but also the focus of external investors and other stakeholders. These contents obviously need to be designed and formulated by the risk management team. The following are two examples of my personal experience.

1.1 The First Example

In early 2010, I left the foreign bank and joined a securities company to engage in risk management work. Soon after, the entire securities industry set off an innovation wave. Especially in the years 2012-2013, I personally participated deeply in innovative businesses such as bond repurchase with pledge, interest rate swaps, Treasury futures, stock agreed repurchase, stock yield swaps, and over-the-counter stock options. I often went to the securities exchange, the China Securities Association, and other external supervision agencies to participate in on-site defense meetings for these innovative businesses. The thrilling and intense scenes of the defense meetings are still fresh in my memory. In addition, with the continuous advancement of the group's corporate and platform process, in addition to the original public fund management company, futures company, and Hong Kong company, a series of subsidiaries such as asset management company, direct investment company, alternative investment company, and investment bank have been established one after another. Strengthening the control over subsidiaries naturally falls within the scope of the company's comprehensive risk management, and I have had more opportunities to become familiar with the various businesses and products of the subsidiaries.

1.2 The Second Example

In early 2015, I joined a rapidly developing trust company to engage in risk management work. It was during a period of innovation and transformation in the trust industry. In 2015 alone, I participated in a variety of new businesses such as asset securitization, accounts receivable factoring, New Third Board funds, public welfare trusts, consumer trusts, Internet finance, photovoltaic industry funds, and investment in the Hong Kong stock IPO, which was quite dazzling. In early May 2016, in order to further strengthen the company's risk management team, a senior employee from the business department, Ms. Zhang, transferred to the risk management team. After working for a month, I asked her about her personal feelings about the risk management work. She excitedly told me, "In the month of working in the risk management department, the number of new businesses and products I have been exposed to has exceeded the total of the past year in the business department."

In 2016, a popular saying in WeChat Moments was: "In the workplace, many people's ten years of work experience is often one year of experience working for ten years." However, this logic is absolutely impossible in risk management, because engaging in risk management work requires a lifetime of effort and learning, and often every day requires accepting new tests and experiencing various trials. Against the backdrop of the continuous reform, opening up, and innovation of China's financial industry, if you are fortunate enough to work solidly in the risk management position for ten years, the ten years of work experience is absolutely genuine and without any water, and personal growth is not a simple linear growth but an exponential growth.

2. Value Two: Working With Excellent Colleagues

Ms. Dong Mingzhu, the chairman of Gree Electric Appliances, clearly mentioned in an interview with "Harvard Business Review" in 2013: "What does the development of a company rely on? Rely on technology? Rely on marketing? No, I think it is the management ability." Similarly, the development of a financial institution also needs to rely on management ability, especially risk management ability! At the same time, whether in business or finance, trust is very important. The success of a financial institution largely depends on the trust of investors, customers, and other stakeholders in the institution's risk management. An excellent financial institution is always accompanied by an outstanding risk management team.

There is a popular online game called "CrossFire" that has a saying: "Not afraid of a god-like opponent, just afraid of a pig-like teammate!" In the risk management team, it is really difficult to meet a pig-like teammate, and meeting a god-like teammate is the norm, after all, "birds of a feather flock together." When I joined the securities company in early 2010, the risk management team had a total of 18 people, including 6 doctors, 8 certified public accountants, and 5 lawyers, and even the colleagues responsible for the development of the risk management system project in the team were also doctors graduated from the computer science major of Shanghai Jiao Tong University. The company's Chief Risk Officer, Mr. Li, once said with great pride: "The proportion of doctors in the risk management team, as well as the proportion of professional certificates, is probably one of the best in the company."

According to social psychology analysis, as a social animal, individuals will gradually align with the group in many aspects such as cognition, judgment, and beliefs during group activities. The saying "You are the average of the five people you spend the most time with" perfectly reflects the important influence of the external environment, especially the team and colleagues, on individuals. During the period of engaging in risk management work, I took advantage of my spare time to successfully obtain the Chartered Financial Analyst (CFA), Certified Public Accountant (CPA), and a doctoral degree, which is largely attributed to the exemplary effect of excellent colleagues at work. At the same time, I also deeply realized that "An excellent team will not let any member of the team fall behind, and the power of a group of excellent people working together is far greater than the sum of the strength of individuals fighting alone."

In addition, I also want to say that people who are engaged in risk management work are usually calm in character, rigorous in behavior, and rational in doing things. I have never seen anyone particularly strange engaged in risk management work. It can be said that the practitioners of risk management are all a group of very lovely and wise elves. Perhaps some people are suspicious, what has created "a god-like teammate in the risk management team?" I think this is due to the financial institution's strict access to risk management talent and extremely high threshold, the following are a few examples.

Example 1: My first risk management job was to be responsible for the risk management of the company's bond investment proprietary business. This position had been vacant for more than a year before I applied, and the company had tried headhunting recommendations, internal recruitment, and other means, but did not meet the right candidates. Even in this case, the company still adhered to the human resource policy of "better absent than misfit."

Example 2: In 2012, the risk management team I was in selected two Peking University graduates from thousands of university graduates, one is an economics doctor and the other is a mathematics master. An important reason for hiring this mathematics master was that the student studied in one of the four famous high schools in Shanghai, the High School Affiliated to East China Normal University.

Example 3: At the trust company I joined in early 2015, the company had a special personnel regulation internally: in addition to the three rounds of interviews by the head of the department, the Chief Risk Officer, and the president, the final employment list needs to be reported to the president's office meeting for collective discussion before it can be decided. The company's strict control over the introduction of risk management talent is even higher than that of the front desk business department head.

Example 4: In 2016, I discussed with the company's Chief Risk Officer about the recruitment of new employees for the risk management team in 2017. I proposed three bottom line requirements for candidates: first, a master's degree or above from well-known domestic and foreign universities; second, at least two of the four professional certificates of Certified Public Accountant, lawyer, Chartered Financial Analyst (CFA), and Financial Risk Manager (FRM); third, more than five years of relevant work experience in well-known domestic and foreign financial institutions or the Big Four international accounting firms.

3. Value Three: Meeting Outstanding Leaders

In April 2015, I had the opportunity to converse with Dr. Li, the CEO of a top 5 asset-scaled public fund company in China. During our exchange, Dr. Li mentioned, "When choosing a job, one must make three selections in sequence: choose an industry with development potential, choose an outstanding enterprise within the industry, and choose an outstanding leader within the enterprise." "The train runs fast, all thanks to the locomotive." Since the beginning of my career in risk management in early 2010, I have been in contact with more than 200 risk management team leaders and Chief Risk Officers from financial institutions. Based on my personal observations,

I have found that these individuals are essentially outstanding leaders in their respective fields. Of course, there are many dimensions to evaluate whether a leader is outstanding, and here I focus on three dimensions: a solid professional background, encouraging employee growth, and having a good vision, which I will elaborate on below.

3.1 Solid Professional Background

If financial work is likened to a dazzling crown, then risk management is the most brilliant pearl on the crown. Risk management involves a multitude of disciplines beyond financial knowledge, including accounting, law, statistics, information technology, and more. In their roles, the leaders of risk management teams and Chief Risk Officers act as mentors and academic leaders in the field of risk management. They often provide team members with guidance and solutions based on their work experience and professional background, sometimes posing incisive questions and unconventional ideas that prompt employees to think deeply. For instance, in the securities company I joined in early 2010, the head of the risk management team, Mr. Wang, is a Ph.D. graduate from Fudan University, and the Chief Risk Officer, Mr. Li, is a post-doctoral fellow from Fudan University. It is common to find risk management leaders with such high academic qualifications in many excellent financial institutions both domestically and internationally.

3.2 Encouraging Employee Growth

An outstanding risk management leader, in addition to having a strong professional background, actively encourages each team member to learn and grow. This includes supporting employees in attending professional training, pursuing higher degrees, and obtaining valuable professional certifications. In September 2012, within the risk management team I was part of, two employees were admitted to doctoral programs.

The team leader made every effort to facilitate their academic journey, such as increasing work time flexibility without affecting their duties. Moreover, since the risk management team does not have the heavy performance assessment indicators like the business team, the leaders of risk management are usually more approachable and have more opportunities to have heart-to-heart conversations with team members, understanding their thoughts about their work and expectations for their future careers. This helps to form a stable and lasting "psychological contract" within the team.

3.3 Having a Good Vision

Leaders in risk management are often visionaries and pioneers with noble aspirations. One might ask, what is a vision? In essence, a vision is a common goal that brings people together to create value. Of course, a vision is feasible, grounded in reality, yet higher than reality without straying too far from it. For risk management, becoming a benchmark in the industry is a relatively realistic vision. After all, risk management in China is still in its infancy, with great potential for future development. Although many risk management tools and methods have been discussed in textbooks, integrating these tools and methods effectively with Chinese financial institutions is a challenging task that cannot be accomplished overnight. This requires a visionary risk management leader to guide the team, adhering to the philosophy of building a tower from sand and a fur coat from foxes, and moving forward towards the goal step by step.

Since graduating with a master's degree in 2005 and stepping into the financial workplace, I have often pondered, "What do I want to do in this life?" Later, whether by accident or fate, I was fortunate to embark on the path of risk management. I gradually realized that risk management is not just a job, but a cause that can be fought for a lifetime!

FROM ZERO TO ONE IN RISK MANAGEMENT

One day in 2018, I found myself sipping coffee at Starbucks with a friend, Mr. Liu, who is a risk control officer. During our conversation, I learned that he was about to move to a newly established financial institution to take on the role of head of the risk management team. I congratulated him, saying, "This is a significant step in your career! However, your previous work was about scaling risk management from '1 to N.' Now, you're about to start from '0 to 1,' which is even more challenging!" With a smile, Mr. Liu admitted the pressure and asked for my advice.

After pondering for a moment, I replied, "The head of a risk management team should be an excellent 'designer,' responsible for the top-level design and conception of the entire risk management system. Based on my experience, the risk management system can be succinctly described as the 'Four Ones Project'—'A set of risk control systems, an Operation Manual, a system platform, and a team of talented individuals.'"

1. A Set Of Risk Control Systems

There is an old Chinese saying, "Without rules, there is no circle." Just as a country's rules are established through laws and regulations, the rules of a financial institution are clarified through systems. Therefore, the objectives of risk management, risk appetite, and tolerance levels, as well as the main methods and tools of risk management, need to be clearly defined in a set of systems and ultimately become the action guide for a financial institution. Of course, it's not about having more systems; they should be formulated based on practical needs, especially those required by regulatory bodies and essential for actual work.

Generally, a set of risk control systems should at least include a "Risk Management Method" document. This document is akin to the constitution of risk management, typically encompassing risk governance structure, risk management strategy, risk appetite, risk limits, risk management policies, and procedures. Objectively speaking, this system is not difficult to draft, as it can refer to external regulatory provisions and similar systems from peers. It is worth noting that the "Comprehensive Risk Management Guidelines for Banking Financial Institutions" released by the China Banking Regulatory Commission in September 2016 is an excellent document that I have read no less than three times. In terms of concept, content, and writing style, it represents the highest standard of risk management regulatory provisions in China and is highly recommended for reference by non-banking financial institutions such as insurance, securities, futures, funds, and trusts.

Additionally, for each type of business, it is usually necessary to formulate separate risk management guidelines. Formulating risk management guidelines for traditional businesses is often straightforward. However, there are real challenges when it comes to innovative businesses. Only by truly understanding and thoroughly grasping innovative businesses can one formulate operational and implementable risk management guidelines; otherwise, the guidelines will be out of touch with reality. In 2012, the securities company where I was working was preparing to launch a brand-new business, the "bond pledge repurchase business with quoted prices." I represented the risk management team and joined the preparatory work group for this new business. Writing the risk management guidelines for this business was a painstaking process, and even a few minutes before going to the Shanghai Stock Exchange to attend the business defense meeting, I was still discussing the specific details of the risk management guidelines with other members of the work group.

Finally, these systems need to be drafted by the risk management department. After the drafting is completed, it is necessary to fully solicit opinions from business departments and other middle and back-office departments (such as the compliance department, finance department, etc.). Of course, reasonable parts of these opinions should be adopted, and unreasonable or inappropriate parts should be given reasons for not being adopted. Then, submit it to the company's management for approval. After approval, it should be issued internally throughout the company.

2. An Operation Manual

Since the system stipulates principled content, there is still a certain gap from specific operations. Therefore, it is also necessary to compile an Operation Manual that transforms each clause of the system into processes and key points in risk management work.

For example, taking the full cycle risk management of a trust plan as an example. In this cycle, it involves a complete chain-like structure of workflow such as project initiation, due diligence, review, contract signing, regulatory filing, mortgage registration, disbursement, post-investment management, profit distribution, maturity liquidation, and risk disposal in case of default. Different departments and positions are involved in each link, and the same department and position will have different work contents and requirements in different links. The materials required in each link are also different, and the working time for each link will also be arranged differently.

From 2006 to 2010, when I was engaged in credit business in a foreign bank, there was a very detailed credit Operation Manual inside the bank. The credit Operation Manual clearly stipulated the various processes and risk control measures involved in credit work, and it was dynamically updated by the risk management department of the head office. At that time, I joked with some colleagues that with this Operation Manual, college graduates could easily do credit approval. As expected, in actual work, there were indeed several graduates who came to the branch directly after graduation to engage in credit approval work.

In February 2010, on my first day of work at the securities company as a risk management professional, the head of the risk management team gave me a compliance and risk management Operation Manual that was more than 500 pages thick. This Operation Manual not only covers various lines of business such as brokerage business, margin trading business, investment banking business, research consulting business, asset management business, and proprietary investment business of the securities company, but also covers every working link of each business as much as possible. It took me a whole week to read this manual completely, and I also referred to it at any time during my work.

Of course, writing a complete risk management Operation Manual is not an easy task, and it is not something that can be done in one day. Because risk management work involves different departments, different positions, different businesses, and different risk control points. At the same time, it is also necessary to consider which processes must be in series and which processes can be parallel to improve work efficiency. Writing an Operation Manual is a time-consuming and labor-intensive huge project, but it is necessary for risk management work. Generally speaking, you can first formulate an Operation Manual for each position within the risk management department, and then gradually expand it into an Operation Manual for the entire risk management department, and finally evolve into an Operation Manual for all types of businesses in the company.

3. An Information System Platform

In 2015, when I was engaged in risk management work in a trust company, I heard about such a true event. There is a medium-sized trust company in China that did not have a risk management information system, and the risk management reports submitted to the regulatory authorities every month were made by hand with Excel forms. Due to the internal personnel changes in the risk management department, the original employee responsible for making the report was transferred to another department, and the work of making the report fell on a new employee who had just graduated. Due to poor handover of work, the monthly regulatory report was returned three times by the regulatory authorities, and it was almost criticized by the regulatory authorities. Since then, the company has made up its mind to establish a risk management information system to achieve automatic generation of various reports.

When I was engaged in risk management work in the securities company, an important task was to take the lead in building the company's risk management information system. Of course, my work was mainly responsible for the design of functional requirements, not involving specific code writing and other development work. Even so, I still have some experience and thinking in the construction of the risk management system.

The risk management information system is not a simple data collection and statistics, but also needs to cover other functions, such as risk monitoring, risk analysis (sensitivity analysis, stress testing, VaR, etc.), risk warning and disposal, risk reporting, and so on. At the same time, in order to ensure the timeliness, accuracy, and completeness of data collection in the risk management information system, it is necessary to connect with other internal systems of the company such as the trading system, clearing system, valuation system, financial system, and external data service providers.

At present, the risk management information systems of most financial institutions are outsourced, and there are very few self-developed ones. The external system developers for cooperation are the key to the entire system construction. Therefore, the first step is to find the right developer. To be honest, there are very few technology companies in China that can really engage in the development of risk management information systems, and the risk management information systems developed by different technology companies are also different, with varying quality and widely varying prices, so it is necessary to compare goods before.

After selecting the developer, we will deal with the software engineers of the developer. To be honest, most software engineers are very professional in IT, but their understanding of finance, especially risk management, is still very superficial. Therefore, it is necessary to clearly require the developer to select excellent and experienced software engineers in advance, and the usual standard is to have developed the same type of risk management information system in at least two financial institutions.

In addition, in the process of system development, in addition to proposing specific, comprehensive, clear, and easy-to-understand demand plans, the risk management team must also fully participate in the system development. Risk managers need to communicate repeatedly with software engineers to ensure that engineers can fully understand. Otherwise, there will be a consequence of "a slight error leads to a big mistake", which not only affects the system development process but also affects the final use of users.

4. A Team Of Talents

In order to prevent the system from becoming an empty paper hanging on the wall, to prevent the Operation Manual from becoming a pile of waste paper locked in the drawer, and to prevent the risk management information system from becoming a work that software engineers appreciate alone, it is necessary to build a strong risk management team to implement it. I believe that the members of a risk management team should include the following three types of personnel.

The first type is professionals with a compound background in finance and finance. These employees can participate in project due diligence, organize and carry out risk inspections for business teams and other middle and back-office functional teams, and can also be responsible for daily risk monitoring. Generally, these employees usually have rich audit work experience in well-known domestic and foreign accounting firms.

The second type is professionals with a compound background in finance and IT. These employees can be responsible for the construction of risk management informatization, responsible for the management of information technology risks, and at the same time, they are also capable of managing risks in quantitative investment business. For example, when I worked in the securities company, the member of the risk management team, Dr. Quan, graduated from Shanghai Jiao Tong University and obtained a doctorate in computer science. Dr. Quan also has many years of work experience in the development of IT systems in a joint-stock commercial bank.

The third type is professionals who understand risk management and have good writing skills. This is because the risk management team needs to write various comprehensive reports regularly and irregularly. The readers of these reports include external regulatory authorities, members of the company's board of directors, members of the company's supervisory board, members of the company's management, etc. For example, when I worked in the securities company, there was a Dr. Zhang in the risk management team who had rich experience in the financial industry. Dr. Zhang's main job is to be responsible for writing various comprehensive reports on risk management, and the professionalism and quality level of the reports are absolutely first-class in the industry.

However, before 2018, there was a serious imbalance in the supply and demand of risk management talents in China. This imbalance is reflected in the total imbalance and structural imbalance. In terms of total imbalance, the number of risk management talents is far from meeting the needs of financial institutions for recruitment. I basically receive calls from headhunters every week. They eagerly recommend various risk management positions to me. In terms of structural imbalance, there are relatively more risk management talents for traditional businesses, such as credit services, while there is a severe shortage of talents for comprehensive risk management and innovative businesses, such as private equity and alternative investments. For instance, in 2016, when I was working in risk management at a trust company, the department was looking to recruit a risk manager responsible for equity investments. The headhunter recommended over 50 candidates, but in the end, none were hired.

From my office, I can see China's tallest building, the

"Shanghai Tower," right outside the window. I often think that risk management is like constructing this skyscraper. Without a solid foundation from 0 to 1, there will be no subsequent growth from 1 to N.

RISK MANAGEMENT NEEDS CREATIVE ELITES

One day in 2018, I happened to see the book "How Google Works," co-authored by Google's chairman and former executives, on the desk of a colleague who had left the company. I spent a few months reading it during my spare time at work. The book focuses on the importance and practical significance of creative elites in the Internet industry. After reading the whole book, I felt enlightened and refreshed, realizing that risk management also needs creative elites. Therefore, this article will discuss this topic. The article is divided into two parts: the first part reveals why risk management needs creative elites, and the second part explores the characteristics of creative elites in risk management work.

1. Why Risk Management Needs Creative Elites

Many readers might feel puzzled when they see the title of this article, wondering if risk management also needs to gather a group of creative elites like the cultural industry. My answer is affirmative. The most direct, simple, and obvious reason is that risk management is an art. In addition to this, I personally believe there are four practical needs.

1.1 Implementing the Concept and Requirements of

Comprehensive Risk Management

Since 2012, Chinese financial regulatory bodies including the China Banking Regulatory Commission, the China Insurance Regulatory Commission, and the China Securities Regulatory Commission have proposed the concept and requirements of "comprehensive risk management." Comprehensive risk management can be considered an original concept in China, as there is no direct equivalent in foreign financial dictionaries. The closest term might be "Enterprise Risk Management." In this sense, China's understanding and requirements for risk management have surpassed those of developed countries. However, it is not difficult to propose a new term; the challenge lies in truly implementing comprehensive risk management in practice. After all, this is an unprecedented and unreferenced bold attempt. To truly achieve comprehensive risk management, creative thinking is required, and creative risk management talents need to be introduced.

1.2 Continuous Introduction of New Financial Products and Services

In 2011, the Chinese securities industry vigorously promoted innovation. The Chief Risk Officer of my securities company, Mr. Li, often stated at meetings: "Under such an innovative backdrop, the company's risk management needs a disruptive reconstruction." At that time, due to my shallow experience in risk management work and the influence of risk management textbooks, I did not seriously consider the meaning of this statement. I simply regarded it as an "astonishing" remark from Mr. Li. At the same time, the entire risk management team of the company lacked creative talents, so the company's risk management did not undergo reconstruction or disruption. I think this has also become a regret in Mr. Li's career. Later, with the continuous enrichment of my risk management experience and the subsequent transformation of China's financial ecology,

I gradually understood the profound meaning behind Mr. Li's words.

1.3 Closer Integration of Industry and Finance, Restructuring of Valuation Systems

During the transition period of China's new and old economic drivers, and the transformation period of China's new economy, new business forms, and new industries, no financial institution can stand aloof. At the same time, Chinese investors are increasingly "fond of the new and tired of the old," and the entire capital market's valuation system is undergoing reconstruction. For example, on January 5, 2017, the Chinese media "Securities Times" published a report titled "Amazon's Market Value Surpasses the Total of Major American Physical Retail Giants," which mentioned that the market value of the American e-commerce giant Amazon has exceeded the total market value of American physical retail enterprises including Walmart. The restructuring of the capital market valuation system inevitably requires corresponding changes to the traditional risk management system. In addition, these emerging industries also have some distinct characteristics from traditional industries. These characteristics include the intangibility of assets (mainly reflected in talents, technology, intellectual property rights), long-term losses, and multi-round financing. In addition, companies in emerging industries are also mixed, and the Matthew effect of the industry is obvious. Therefore, the risks in emerging industries are higher and more concealed, which also requires an innovative risk management system.

1.4 The Financial Industry is Using Creativity to Guide Work

In January 2017, the Chinese edition of "Harvard Business Review" published an article titled "The Key to Innovation: Talent or Method?" The article mentioned the distinctive innovation process of American banks - research and experimentation, then converted into services. For example, some branches within the bank are arranged to be creative laboratories to test those "good ideas that have a great impact and can support many different experiments but are small enough not to let the entire business fall into crisis." Although the article did not mention specific creative content (probably considering commercial secrets), creativity must be proposed by people, and risk management must be embedded in the innovation process. At the same time, I also believe that similar innovation processes will appear in Chinese financial institutions.

2. Characteristics Of Creative Risk Management Talents

Some people might say, "Isn't the characteristic of creative elites to have extraordinary imagination and creativity?" This statement is both right and wrong. It is right because the main internal characteristics of creative elites are indeed these. It is wrong because these characteristics are internal. Internal characteristics are not easy to observe and perceive. However, according to my personal experience, I have found that creative elites in risk management work have some obvious and common external characteristics. Through these external characteristics, it is possible to infer the internal characteristics with a higher probability, which is like the Bayesian rule in statistics - inferring the probability of the occurrence of the underlying causes by observing the phenomena.

These external characteristics include a young mindset, extensive reading, focused thinking, broad expertise, and a pragmatic style.

2.1 A Young Mindset

A person's age is divided into physiological age and psychological age. Physiological age is objective and irreversible. However, psychological age can always be young, always at 18 years old. Psychological age determines a person's mindset. Mindset determines a person's work state. Creative elites in risk management have a young mindset, mainly reflected in two aspects.

First, embracing new things. Creative elites will maintain a continuous sense of freshness towards new things and are brave to try and experience. I personally think that whether you are 20 years old or 80 years old, if you are no longer interested in new things, it means that you are really old. I have a very good risk control officer friend, Mr. Zhang, who is a post-70s generation. Although he is not young, he always gives people the vitality and sunshine of being 18 years old. For example, when the online live broadcast platform was just launched in 2015, Mr. Zhang personally experienced online live broadcasting. Mr. Zhang sometimes buys a drone for his own entertainment and will take a sudden overseas trip. In fact, the process of experiencing new things is the process of understanding new business forms, new models, and new blue oceans more comprehensively, and of course, it is also the process of better recognizing and controlling the risks behind new business forms and new models.

Second, passion for work. In risk management work, creative elites will be full of passion for their work. They are not only 100% invested in their work but often 200% invested. At the same time, creative elites are very persistent in their careers, not just a whim, and not just a three-minute heat. According to my long-term observation in the workplace, people who can maintain a lasting passion for a job are often young in spirit. Otherwise, if a person is just "doing a day's work and hitting a day's bell" or "fishing for two days and drying the net for three days," it means that the mentality has aged. If a person is fickle in their work and frequently jumps, it means that this person's mentality is too naive.

2.2 Extensive Reading

The second external characteristic of creative elites in risk management work is a love for reading, and the content of reading is very extensive. On the one hand, whether it is the financial industry or the real economy, the iteration speed is getting faster and faster. If you don't insist on reading, you will not keep up with the pace of the development of the times. On the other hand, there are often many common characteristics between different disciplines, and extensive reading will make people learn by analogy and think actively. For creative elites in risk management work, reading usually includes the following three aspects.

First, reading various financial newspapers and periodicals. Macroeconomics, meso-industry, micro-subjects, and legal policies are all dynamically changing. Mastering these changes is the most fundamental and important thing for risk management. Maybe a business with a lower risk today will become a business with a higher risk after a few days or months. Therefore, creative elites in risk management will read a large number of financial newspapers and periodicals every day, grasping the key points of risk and the core of control in the dynamically changing economic and financial environment.

Second, reading various research reports. In-depth understanding and learning of the industry usually require the help of industry research reports issued by domestic and foreign investment institutions, securities companies, research institutes, etc. Through these reports, one can have a more in-depth and comprehensive understanding of the development of the industry. A comprehensive grasp of regulatory policies and laws and regulations usually requires thematic reports provided by professional consulting institutions, law firms, etc.

Third, reading various new books and miscellaneous books. Whether it is reading various financial newspapers and periodicals or various research reports, the purpose is to help enhance the depth of risk management work. Reading various new books and miscellaneous books is to help broaden the breadth of risk management work. Of course, different people will have reading preferences. Generally speaking, creative elites in risk management will choose to read some non-financial books such as philosophy, history, astronomy, science, and sociology to broaden their horizons.

2.3 Focused Thinking

In risk management work, creative inspiration is inseparable from focused thinking. This kind of thinking includes both individual contemplation and extensive discussions with others.

Contemplation is omnipresent and can be done anytime, anywhere. It is not only during work hours but also in spare time. It is not only in the office but also on the way to work, during business trips, and at one's residence. At the same time, it is necessary to be good at recording one's thoughts to capture the moment of birth of every inspiration. When I was working at the securities company, the chairman of the company, Mr. Pan, shared some of his personal habits with the employees. Mr. Pan always carries a few pieces of white paper and a pen in his pocket, ready to record his thoughts at any time. He also keeps a notebook and pen beside his pillow, ready to write down any thoughts that come to him before sleep or upon waking. These habits are probably one of the main reasons why Mr. Pan was able to rise from a grassroots employee to the chairman of the company!

There is a saying: "You have an idea, I have an idea, and after we discuss, we will form a third or even more ideas." I once read an article whose core idea was that the birth of the U.S. Constitution was the result of extensive discussions and even fierce debates. Discussion is not only very important but also indispensable. After all, even the smartest person may overlook something when thinking. Therefore, creative elites in risk management understand the importance of opening the door to discussions to everyone. They not only discuss within the team but also with business teams and external analysts, accountants, lawyers, and other experts. After repeated and multiple rounds of discussions, innovations and ideas in risk management work can become more practical and feasible.

2.4 Broad Expertise

Risk management is by no means an isolated and simple science, but an interdisciplinary discipline that spans multiple disciplines. In July 2021, Professor Hu from the International College of Renmin University of China sought my opinion on the construction of China's risk management discipline system. At that time, I wrote a written material, suggesting that risk management should at least cover essential professional knowledge such as finance, mathematics, statistics, finance, accounting, and law.

Creative elites in risk management are first and foremost people who have a solid and comprehensive grasp of these professional knowledge areas. Mastery of these professional knowledge areas requires a long-term specialized learning and rigorous systematic training process. After all, risk management is not a child's play, and without the accumulation of these professional knowledge areas, the entire risk management work would lose its foundation. Without the accumulation of these professional knowledge areas, there can be no innovation and breakthrough in risk management work. Without the inheritance of these professional knowledge areas, those seemingly innovative and new ideas in risk management will only be eye-catching but useless vases, or even essentially a complete deception.

Mastering the necessary professional knowledge is enough to reach the standard of creative elites? The answer is "far from it." Because risk management is also a management science, and the process of managing risks is actually a process of managing people. And risk management is about managing the most intelligent, most thoughtful, and most unmanageable group of elites in the financial industry (such as traders, investment managers, etc.). In the work, it is necessary to communicate risks and control measures with these managers, and to make these managers truly accept management and constraints from the heart. Therefore, for creative elites, they often also have knowledge and skills in other disciplines such as management science, psychology, linguistics, and behavioral science, so as to ultimately apply creativity and innovation to practical risk management work.

2.5 Practical Work Style

Talking the talk is easy, but walking the walk is the real skill. Many things are easy to say but hard to do. Knowing is easy, but doing is difficult, especially for risk management work. However, many people often confuse creative elites with those who are fanciful and boastful. In fact, this is a big mistake. Creative elites also have a very important external characteristic, which is a down-to-earth work style and strong execution ability. Otherwise, it is impossible to implement their creative ideas and innovative thoughts into risk management work.

On the one hand, creative elites will form their own set of working methods. They will first design risk management work into a task book, arrange a timetable, and plan a roadmap. Then they will proceed step by step and gradually. They will not be rash, nor will they be conservative. In the process of work, they will often look back and summarize experiences and lessons in time. At the same time, they will dynamically assess the external environment and objective conditions, and make changes and adjustments to the work when necessary.

On the other hand, creative elites will recognize that risk management work is not a one-person job, but a team job. No matter how strong a person's ability is, how high the efficiency is, and how busy the work is, the effect and results are very limited. Therefore, in addition to their own work, they will also stimulate the enthusiasm of team members and mobilize everyone's creativity to work together and work together. Turn their creative ideas into the team's action guide. Turn their innovative ideas into the team's work direction. Finally, achieve the best work results and the greatest work results.

Are there such creative elites in risk management in China? My answer is definitely yes! Are there many? I'm afraid not many! Therefore, financial institutions need the management to have a discerning eye to find them, to build a platform to incubate them, and to use a set of mechanisms to retain them.

HOW TO BUILD A LEARNING-ORIENTED RISK MANAGEMENT TEAM

One day in September 2019, I received a call from my friend Mr. Shen, a Chief Risk Officer. During the call, Mr. Shen complained that the risk management work he was responsible for did not receive the attention it deserved from the company's management, and the risk management team lacked a sense of presence and pride. After listening to Mr. Shen's complaints, my first reaction as a peer was that we should not blame the company; the problem might very well lie within the risk management team itself. After inquiring in detail, I found out that the real reason was the lack of professionalism in Mr. Shen's risk control team. After all, the core of risk management work is "people". The professionalism of a risk management team comes from continuous learning and persistent research. Only when the risk management team makes a difference in the company can it gain a respected status. Therefore, this article would like to discuss my personal thoughts on how to build a learning-oriented risk management team.

1. Using Professional Certificates As A Lever

Risk management is a highly specialized management task. At the same time, against the backdrop of the great transformation and innovation in China's financial industry, the business, products, and industries that risk management work can touch are extremely broad. In my personal view, the risk management team should be the team with the strongest learning ability and the highest willingness to learn in a financial institution.

For each member of the risk management team, they should be expert generalists, needing to master a comprehensive range of professional knowledge and skills in finance, finance, statistics, law, etc. In the team I lead, I actively encourage each member to take exams for professional certificates with strong expertise, high gold content, and low pass rates, such as Certified Public Accountant (CPA), Chartered Financial Analyst (CFA), and Financial Risk Manager (FRM). I personally set an example and take the lead. After all, participating in these certificate exams can help one to have a systematic and comprehensive grasp of financial knowledge in the shortest possible time.

Of course, at the beginning, there will inevitably be some team members who do not understand my initiative. Among them, a team member, Ms. Lu, took the initiative to complain to me, "Leader, you have these certificates because you are a top student, but I am not you, I guess I can't pass the exam even if I take it!" I replied to Ms. Lu with three sentences. The first sentence is "How can you know you can do it without trying!" The second sentence is "Getting these certificates is not as difficult as you think. I also took the exam while working and successfully obtained these certificates." The third sentence is "One cannot only consider the current self, but also plan for the self of 10 years later." Ms. Lu finally accepted my advice, not only passed the certificate examination smoothly, but also the work state and learning state are getting better and better. In addition, Ms. Lu's success also inspired the whole team to learn and take the exam actively!

However, as the person in charge of the risk management team, in addition to using oneself as a role model to stimulate the team members' enthusiasm for learning, it is more necessary to seek breakthroughs in the employee assessment mechanism. Therefore, I have repeatedly suggested to the company's management to add points for obtaining specific professional certificates (such as CPA, CFA, FRM, etc.) in the assessment of risk management team members. This establishes a long-term mechanism for employees to continuously obtain professional certificates.

2. Using Interactive Learning As A Link

As the person in charge of the risk management team, I also actively use the company's relevant resources to build a risk management sharing and learning platform. This platform can include three sub-platforms: one is the internal sharing and learning platform of the risk management team, the second is the sharing and learning platform between the risk management team and the business team, and the third is the sharing and learning platform within the same industry. The following is a detailed introduction and analysis.

2.1 Internal Sharing and Learning Platform of the Risk Management Team

In order to improve work efficiency, there are different divisions of labor among the members of the risk management team. For example, commercial banks usually divide according to the different industries of the customers. Securities companies often divide according to different business lines such as proprietary business, asset management business, investment banking business, brokerage business, and margin trading business. In public fund management companies, they often divide according to different types of products such as equity, fixed income, and financial derivatives. Therefore, a good atmosphere of mutual learning and sharing can be formed through regular internal team training.

For example, in 2016, asset securitization was a hot topic in China's financial market. A training institution invited several experts to hold a training session on asset securitization. Since the training session had limited seats and high training fees, the trust company I was in only arranged for one risk manager, Ms. Fang, to attend. After the training session, Ms. Fang made more than 100 pages of PPT and shared it with the entire company's risk management team for more than 3 hours. During the sharing process, the discussion within the risk management team was very intense, which ultimately greatly improved the entire team's understanding and cognition of asset securitization.

2.2 Sharing and Learning Platform between Risk Management Team and Business Team

Although risk management work requires independence and objectivity, it does not hinder the smooth communication and interaction between the risk management team and the business team. According to my personal experience and observation, the more smooth, close, and frequent the communication between the risk management team and the business team, the higher the effectiveness and recognition of risk management will often be. The question is, how to build such a platform?

Firstly, financial institutions can hold special seminars on new products and new businesses internally. Since the business team is at the forefront of the market, it is relatively easy to obtain the first-hand information and comprehensive information about new products and new businesses in the financial industry. Given the time lag in information transmission and the potential asymmetry of information, the risk management team may be half a beat slower in the rhythm of information acceptance, and there is also a dilemma of insufficient information grasp. Therefore, financial institutions hold relevant special seminars to promote the business team and the risk management team to sit together and conduct a 360-degree comprehensive analysis and evaluation of new products and new businesses. Such special seminars are a very rare learning opportunity for the risk management team.

Secondly, the rotation mechanism between business personnel and risk control personnel. Based on my personal observation over the years, I have found an interesting rule. In financial institutions, outstanding business team leaders or executives in charge of business often have certain risk management work experience, and excellent risk control officers will have several years of business work experience. Therefore, it is necessary to establish a two-way interactive mechanism for business personnel to rotate to the risk management team and risk control personnel to rotate to the business team within the company. Since business personnel have been working on the front line for a long time, the starting point and destination of considering problems are often how to enhance the company's market competitiveness and profitability. Therefore, the rotation of business personnel to the risk management team will bring some new concepts and thinking; similarly, since risk control personnel have the professional habit of examining business from a risk perspective, the rotation of risk control personnel to the business team will effectively improve the level of front-line risk control management. The rotation time can be controlled between 3 months and half a year, and it would be better if there is a clear system within the company to regulate the rotation work.

Finally, think and study from the other's perspective.

Thinking from the other's perspective is relatively easy to understand, that is, the risk management team needs to consider risk management issues from the perspective of business development when analyzing and reviewing business, and the business team needs to think about business expansion issues from the perspective of risk management. But how can we achieve research from the other's perspective? In fact, in my view, research from the other's perspective is an upgraded version of thinking from the other's perspective. For example, after the business team successfully completes a new product, they can look back. That is, they play the role of the risk management team and comprehensively sort out and summarize the new product from the perspective of risk management, and form written materials to share with other business teams and the risk management team. Similarly, after the risk management team reviews a new product, they can play the role of the business team, think about the product from the perspective of the company's future business development or even strategic development, and propose specific suggestions to enhance the value of the risk management team within the company.

2.3 Sharing and Learning Platform within the Same Industry

I always believe that the theory of risk management is thin, but the practice of risk management is rich. Within the same financial format (such as banking, trust, insurance, securities, etc.), different financial institutions have differences in market positioning, business focus, profit model, etc. The risk management practices of different institutions are also formed with their own characteristics. Strengthening the exchange of risk management within the same industry is essential.

The same industry exchange mentioned here can have two levels: one is the exchange within the same type of financial format, that is, the exchange between institutions of the same type of financial format. The second is the exchange between different types of financial formats, such as the exchange between commercial banks and insurance companies.

2.3.1 Risk Management Exchange within the Same Small Industry

In fact, China's regulatory authorities and industry self-regulatory organizations hold training sessions, seminars, or forums on risk management every year. These activities themselves are very good platforms for risk management exchange. Of course, due to the large number of institutions attending these activities and the different initial intentions of the participants, it may not be very ideal to use these activities for in-depth and comprehensive industry exchange.

A better alternative is point-to-point visits. Such exchanges are often more comprehensive and thorough. Generally, you can look for institutions with their own business characteristics, after all, these institutions will also have their own unique insights in risk management. Such industry exchanges can collide with many sparks of thought. Here is an example. In 2016's Chinese trust industry, Huabao Trust formed a unique approach in the capital market business, and Anxin Trust had its own comparative advantage in the field of real estate equity investment. Therefore, in that year, I led the risk management team to visit these two trust companies in turn, carried out comprehensive and in-depth exchanges on trust company risk management, and achieved very good results. Of course, point-to-point industry exchanges require a certain amount of manpower and time, generally, it can be carried out once every quarter or half a year.

2.3.2 Risk Management Exchange among Different Industries

With the domestic financial industry entering the era of mixed operation and pan-asset management, the risks faced by financial institutions are becoming more and more diversified, and the risk control exchange between different industries is bound to be a trend.

Generally speaking, commercial banks and trust companies have been engaged in financing business for a long time, so they have rich experience in credit risk management. Securities companies and public fund management companies are deeply involved in the capital market, and have formed a relatively mature system in market risk management. Insurance companies profit from the mismatch of asset and liability duration, and thus have unique practices in liquidity risk management. In addition, with the increasing number of financial holding companies in China, the mother company's consolidated risk management of holding different licensed financial institutions is also gradually maturing.

To build an outstanding learning-oriented risk management team, one must not be limited to the financial format in which they are located. It is necessary to look at the entire financial industry, actively go out, learn from others' strengths and characteristics, and transform them into the team's own professional capabilities, work ideas, and practical methods through "taking and using."

EMOTIONAL INTELLIGENCE IN RISK MANAGEMENT

At the end of 2017, while I was engaged in risk management at a financial holding group, we welcomed a new Chief Risk Officer, Ms. Shi. Ms. Shi has a catchphrase for her work: "Risk management is a strong physique plus a flexible posture." The "strong physique" represents the various professional knowledge required in risk management work, while "flexible posture" implies the emotional intelligence (EQ) needed in the work. Some risk management practitioners have the misconception that "as long as one can become the most professional person in the room, risk management work will be smooth sailing." Undoubtedly, risk management requires strong and comprehensive professional knowledge. However, risk management is still a management job; in addition to knowing what to do, one must also understand how to do it and how to carry it out effectively.

Emotional intelligence (EQ) was first proposed by John Mayer and Peter Salovey, two American psychologists, in 1990. Daniel Goleman, a Ph.D. in psychology from Harvard University, published the book "Emotional Intelligence" in 1995. Since then, the term has become the most popular and fashionable term in the field of management. Daniel Goleman believes that "emotional intelligence is the key to determining whether life is successful or not." In my personal view, emotional intelligence is also key to determining the success of risk management work. Based on my professional experience and various observations at work, this article discusses four aspects of content, in order: emotional intelligence in communication with regulatory authorities, emotional intelligence in working with company leaders, emotional intelligence in getting along with business teams, and emotional intelligence in team internal cooperation.

1. Emotional Intelligence In Communication With Regulatory Authorities

From 2010 to 2014, when I was engaged in risk management work at a securities company, my job responsibilities included serving as a liaison for communication with external regulatory authorities. At first, I didn't understand why the leadership chose me for this important role. Later, I found out that because I had previously worked in the front-line credit business of a foreign bank, my communication and coordination skills should have reassured the leadership. I have held this liaison role for several years, and overall, the regulatory authorities have been very satisfied with me. In terms of emotional intelligence in communication with regulatory authorities, I personally summarize the following three points.

1.1 Sincerity in Communication with Regulatory Authorities

It is often heard in the financial industry that some people comment, "External regulatory authorities are like cats, and financial institutions are like mice; regulation is actually a game between cats and mice." Such a statement is obviously absurd. After all, the financial industry is an industry that operates and manages risks. Financial institutions need government strict regulation while exercising self-discipline. Otherwise, the U.S.

subprime mortgage crisis is a bloody lesson. In communication with external regulatory authorities, it is necessary to always adhere to the principle of "sincerity" and never play hide-and-seek games in front of regulation. Sincerity here mainly includes being honest about the risks found and being genuine in the rectification of risk hidden dangers.

1.1.1 Be Frank About the Risks Found

"The Golden River flows on and on, and there is always another heaven beyond the horizon." A financial institution will inevitably encounter more or less problems and risks during its development process, and it is unrealistic to expect to solve them once and for all. Refusing to accept reality is often the biggest challenge faced by a company, a financial institution. To overcome this challenge, the only effective way is to face it frankly, instead of looking for excuses.

Regulatory authorities regulate many financial institutions at the same time, which means they supervise a multitude of financial institutions. Many risk points and hidden dangers within a financial institution have universality and commonality in the industry, and the information mastered by regulatory authorities is often more comprehensive and extensive. "There are always mountains beyond the mountains, the sky beyond the sky, and people beyond people." Expecting to deal with external supervision by concealment, prevarication, and deception will usually end up being clever by half, losing more than gaining, and hurting oneself with one's own actions.

External supervision can discover some blind spots in the daily operations of financial institutions, better improve their own management, especially risk management, and thus promote their stable development and stable operation. Therefore, whether it is internal self-inspection of the company or on-site inspection by external regulatory authorities, I always welcome it with open arms.

Let's take a real example. In 2011, the securities company where I was located was selected by the China Securities Regulatory Commission (CSRC) as one of the few securities companies in the industry to be inspected. This inspection was led by the Shanghai Securities Regulatory Office of the CSRC (referred to as "Shanghai Office") and was a comprehensive inspection of the company. The inspection work was divided into two stages: the first stage was a two-month internal self-inspection of the company, and the second stage was a three-month on-site inspection by the Shanghai Office. During this inspection, I was fortunate to be the leader of the first stage and participated in the writing of the self-inspection work report. A total of dozens of risks were found in the self-inspection stage, all of which were written into the self-inspection work report. This self-inspection work report was submitted to the person in charge of the Shanghai Office at the beginning of the second stage of work, and after reading it carefully, the person in charge expressed his approval of the company's self-inspection work. In the following years, many securities companies have come to learn how to deal with inspections, and I have passed on the "principle of sincerity" to my peers in the exchange.

1.1.2 Sincere Rectification of Discovered Risks

Now that potential risks have been identified, the next step is rectification. If we do not find ways to rectify them, the problems and hidden dangers will always be there and will not disappear or evaporate automatically. Under certain circumstances, small risks can gradually lead to huge man-made disasters, such as the bill fraud cases that occurred in many commercial banks in China in the first half of 2017, which is a bloody lesson. The principle of "it's not too late to mend the pen when the sheep are lost" is understood and spoken by everyone. However, rectification is also an art, and there is no standard answer. Financial institutions can choose to rectify one by one, or to learn from one example and deal with three;

they can choose "surgical" rectification or "Chinese medicine conditioning" rectification. But no matter what, we need to sincerely rectify the problems and risks that have been found.

Still using the inspection mentioned earlier as an example. After nearly three months of on-site inspections, compared with the problems found during the company's self-inspection, the Shanghai Office still found more and finer risks. Of course, some of the problems were expected, but more problems were unexpected. For the problems found in the inspection, the company's risk management team and the internal audit team were responsible for corresponding each risk to the relevant responsible department, implementing them to the corresponding responsible person, and clarifying specific rectification measures and timetables. At the same time, the subsequent rectification situation was also included in the company's regular risk spot checks and annual audit inspections, and the completion of rectification was included in the performance assessment of departments and individuals. A year later, the Shanghai Office re-inspected the subsequent rectification situation. After the re-inspection was completed, the person in charge of the Shanghai Office said that the company's implementation of rectification was in place, and the entire inspection work was finally concluded satisfactorily.

1.2 Seek Full Understanding from Regulatory Authorities

"The onlookers see most of the game" may not be applicable to the financial industry. After all, the financial industry usually gathers the best talents in the whole society. Therefore, "the insiders are clear, and the onlookers are confused" is a common situation. The process of communicating with external regulatory authorities is also a process of letting regulatory authorities understand the business and risk management of financial institutions. Only by letting regulatory authorities truly and fully understand the business and risk management work of financial institutions can a positive and harmonious interaction between regulators and the regulated be ultimately achieved. Otherwise, there will be a situation of "talking at cross purposes" in the communication between the two parties, increasing various friction costs, and ultimately not only wasting regulatory resources but also having a certain negative impact on the operation of financial institutions and the entire industry. I personally think that seeking the understanding of external regulatory authorities is mainly aimed at two aspects: innovative business and risk management.

1.2.1 Seek Regulatory Authorities' Understanding of Innovative Business

According to my personal observation, regulatory authorities have a relatively comprehensive understanding of traditional business, on-site and standardized products. However, with the acceleration of China's financial reform and innovation, more and more innovative businesses, off-site products, and non-standardized products continue to emerge. Since regulatory authorities are not on the front line of business and have not fully participated in product design, they may also be somewhat confused and unclear about innovative and complex products. Therefore, the risk management team of financial institutions has the responsibility to seek the understanding of regulatory authorities for innovative businesses.

Take an example. At the beginning of 2013, the personnel from the Financial Stability Department of the Shanghai Headquarters of the People's Bank of China came to the securities company where I worked for research. The theme of the research was "Innovation in the Securities Industry and Systemic Financial Risks." The company's risk management team attached great importance to this research. The risk management team, together with the team responsible for promoting innovative business, carefully prepared presentation documents and arranged for the person in charge of the innovative business to accompany and explain throughout the process. During the nearly one-day research, not only was a detailed and comprehensive introduction to the innovative business conducted, but the various risks faced by the business and the risk management measures taken were also explained one by one, and relevant questions were answered truthfully. At the end of the research, the leader of the Financial Stability Department shook our hands and said, "After listening to your detailed and comprehensive introduction, our worries and doubts before coming have been basically dispelled. Overall, I personally feel that the business and product innovation in the securities industry will not bring obvious impact and influence to the systemic risk of the entire financial market."

1.2.2 Seek Regulatory Authorities' Understanding of Risk Management

Although the risk management team of financial institutions often deals with regulatory authorities, due to information asymmetry, regulatory authorities may not fully understand the content of the risk management work of financial institutions. In the first half of 2018, I had an exchange with Mr. Liu, the Chief Risk Officer of a financial institution. Mr. Liu had worked in regulatory authorities for a long time and also admitted that when he was working in regulatory authorities, he felt that risk management work was not difficult or complicated. However, when he is now personally engaged in risk management work, he suddenly found that his previous understanding of risk management was rather narrow and superficial.

Every time when regulatory authorities come to the company for on-site inspections, I will look for various opportunities to popularize and publicize risk management knowledge to the inspectors. I not only introduce what the company's risk management team is doing and why it is necessary to do so, but also tell them about the limitations, gradualness, and long-term nature of risk management itself. In addition, I will also "be a good teacher" and recommend some risk management books and even professional risk management exams to the inspectors. One day in the summer of 2019, I had lunch with several people who had dealt with regulatory authorities before. Many of them have successively left regulatory authorities and joined financial institutions in recent years, serving as Chief Risk Officers or heads of risk management departments. They are very grateful for the popularization and publicity of risk management that I had done during the on-site inspections, which helped them to fully understand risk management and enabled them to quickly integrate into their new roles and realize their self-worth.

1.3 Actively Mobilize Company Leaders When Necessary

Sometimes, in front of regulatory authorities, ordinary employees of the risk management team of financial institutions are often "insignificant". The same sentence, spoken by ordinary employees and company leaders, will definitely have different effects and impacts. Some important words, key words, if they can be spoken by the company's leaders, especially the top leaders, will be very weighty. Therefore, in the communication process with regulatory authorities, it is necessary to mobilize the company's leaders when necessary. There are two major benefits to doing this: on the one hand, it allows the company's management to clearly and truly grasp the risks that the company may currently face and the specific situation of the risks, which is convenient for the future development of risk management work. On the other hand, it allows regulatory authorities to truly feel the company's high attention to risk management work, and ultimately achieve the effect of "using four twos to move a thousand kilograms".

Here is an example about anti-money laundering. In the second half of 2010, the Anti-Money Laundering Office of the

Shanghai Branch of the People's Bank of China established an inspection team to conduct a one-month on-site inspection of the anti-money laundering work of the securities company where I was. At that time, the entire securities industry had not been carrying out anti-money laundering work for a long time, coupled with a lack of professional anti-money laundering talent teams and lack of work experience, so during the entire inspection process, the inspection team found some deficiencies and weak links in the company's anti-money laundering work.

When the inspection was nearing the end, the company's risk management team promptly reported to Chairman Mr. Pan on the anti-money laundering on-site inspection. Mr. Pan attached great importance to this and went to the Shanghai Branch of the People's Bank of China in person the next day. Due to the urgency and without an appointment with the leaders of the Shanghai Branch in advance, and coincidentally, the branch was holding a leadership team meeting. Mr. Pan could only take advantage of the break in the meeting to briefly meet with the leaders of the Shanghai Branch. Mr. Pan was straightforward and very sincere in admitting the company's shortcomings and problems in the anti-money laundering work. At the same time, Mr. Pan solemnly promised that the company would thoroughly rectify the relevant issues found in the inspection in the shortest possible time, and will continue to pay close attention to anti-money laundering work in the future. Finally, the leaders of the Shanghai Branch were deeply moved and also expressed a certain degree of recognition for the company's previous anti-money laundering work. He was pleased that the company's chairman could fully understand and fully support the anti-money laundering work, and also put forward some constructive suggestions for the company's future anti-money laundering work. Since then, Mr. Pan has always paid high attention to anti-money laundering work. The company has also won many honors for advanced units and individuals in the anti-money laundering work of financial institutions in the

Shanghai area.

2. Emotional Intelligence In Working With Corporate Executives

In the second half of 2018, I had lunch with Mr. Feng, the head of the risk management department of a trust company. During the meal, Mr. Feng poured out his troubles. The reason was that in the first half of the year, the company he worked for carried out its biennial salary adjustment for all employees. The monthly salaries of the heads of other departments increased more or less, but Mr. Feng's monthly salary did not increase at all. I asked, "Is the salary increase of each department head discussed collectively by the company's senior executives?" The answer was affirmative. Mr. Feng's daily work intensity and pressure are very high, and working overtime until midnight can be said to be a common occurrence. But it seems that only hard work is done without credit, and the risk management work has not been affirmed by the company's senior management. It is likely that Mr. Feng's experience is not an isolated case. Since there are no obvious quantifiable indicators for evaluating risk management work, how the risk management team works with corporate executives requires emotional intelligence. In this regard, I plan to analyze from the following four dimensions. In addition, the corporate executives discussed here do not include the Chief Risk Officer. After all, the Chief Risk Officer and the risk management team belong to the same "trench," and the Chief Risk Officer is very clear about the work content and intensity of the risk management team.

2.1 Finding the Positioning of the Risk Management Team

The book "Positioning" written by Al Ries and Jack Trout clearly proposes the concept of "positioning" and bluntly points out the important value and practical significance of positioning in marketing and management. Financial institutions are enterprises with the purpose of making a profit. Due to different divisions of labor, financial institutions are divided into different teams or departments, and the risk management team must have a clear and clear positioning in its work. Otherwise, risk management work will be less effective and may even be counterproductive.

2.1.1 Defining the Boundary of Responsibilities

In the positioning of the risk management team, the first thing is the positioning of responsibilities. Based on my personal observation, for most financial institutions, the risk management team should not be a "decision-making team" but a "staff team." The main responsibilities can be summarized as follows: First, fully reveal the risks and put forward reasonable and operable risk management suggestions; second, promptly convey relevant information to the company's decision-making layer; third, ensure that the decision-making layer has fully understood the related risks and risk management suggestions, and has also fully understood the possible consequences. The risk management team should neither be absent nor overstep. The financial industry itself is a high-risk industry, and risk management work is a high-risk job in a high-risk industry. Therefore, finding the right positioning and clarifying responsibilities is also a form of career protection for members of the risk management team.

2.1.2 Enhancing the Height of Thinking

"To see a thousand miles, you must ascend one more floor." The risk management team needs to think about risk management issues from the height of the company's management and even the entire industry, which is the positioning of problem thinking. Of course, achieving this is by no means an easy task. The risk management team needs to delve into the latest products and businesses in the industry, actively study the industries that the company is participating in and planning to participate in, and closely follow the dynamics of the main trading counterparts. Only in this way can the risk management team stand high and see far, and can the risk management work be recognized by the management and reflect the inherent value of risk management work. For example, when I worked in a trust company in 2015, I was fortunate to participate in the company's first asset securitization product with financing lease as the basic asset. I combined theoretical learning with practical experience and wrote an article. This article analyzed the advantages of trust companies in carrying out asset securitization business from the perspective of the trust industry, the potential risks faced, and how to effectively control the related risks. This article was not only forwarded by the WeChat public account of the China Trust Industry Association but also unanimously affirmed by the company's management, effectively enhancing the status of the risk management team in the company.

2.1.3 Combining the Actual Situation of the Company

Risk management is an art, with no standard answers or unchanging paradigms. However, risk management must be combined with the current situation and actual situation of the company, emphasizing the effectiveness of the work and requiring a certain degree of foresight, while absolutely not being too advanced or following trends, which is the positioning of the work thinking. Here is a counterexample. During my tenure in the trust company's risk management work, the person in charge of the risk management department, Mr. Zhou, had been engaged in risk modeling and rating work for a long time before joining the company. Mr. Zhou was eager to replicate the practices of other companies to this company and invited me to try to establish an internal quantitative risk rating model for each trust product and each trading counterpart. The company also recruited senior analysts from credit rating companies and several interns for this purpose. After several months of unremitting efforts by everyone, the first draft of the rating plan was formed. However, when the company's president reviewed the plan, it was shelved. There are many reasons behind this, and the most important one is that this rating plan did not conform to the company's situation at the time, and thus lost its practical significance and value.

2.2 Maintaining the Independence of the Risk Management Team

Steve Jobs, the founder of Apple Inc., once said, "Don't let the noise of others' opinions drown out your own inner voice." Independence and objectivity are the core values and codes of conduct for the risk management team. This requires the team to base its risk analysis, assessment, and judgment on its own professionalism and conscience in risk management work, and to be objective and fair. Risk management should not be interfered with or influenced by external factors, especially not by the company's senior executives, especially the top leader. Only in this way can the risk management team be free from guilt, live a carefree life every day, and sleep peacefully every night. At the same time, this is also a loyalty to the noble profession of risk management and to one's employer. Here are two real-life examples.

2.2.1 The First Case

In 2009, when I was engaged in credit business in a foreign bank, the bank's chairman, Dr. Lee, recommended a Japanese-funded enterprise with financing needs to the Shanghai branch where I was. This Japanese-funded enterprise applied for unsecured, unguaranteed pure credit loans to the Shanghai branch. Although this Japanese-funded enterprise has a long history in operation and has a certain reputation and influence in its industry, the enterprise's debt-to-asset ratio is obviously high, and the short-term debt repayment pressure is relatively large. After the risk management team of the Shanghai branch evaluated it, it was considered that the enterprise did not meet the bank's credit risk standards, and the loan application was ultimately rejected by the bank's credit committee. The Shanghai branch's president, Mr. Nie, informed Dr. Lee of the approval result and reasons of this loan by email. Dr. Lee not only accepted the final result with pleasure but also fully affirmed the due diligence of the Shanghai branch's risk management team.

2.2.2 The Second Case

In the first half of 2016, the trust company where I worked was preparing to invest in a privately-owned wealth management company headquartered in Shanghai. It happened that the actual controller of this wealth management company, Mr. Lu, happened to be an MBA classmate of our company's president, Mr. Liu. The two have a close personal relationship, and the two companies also have a business cooperation relationship. Once, when Mr. Lu visited our trust company, he mentioned that he was considering attracting external shareholders to expand the capital scale. Mr. Liu immediately expressed his hope to invest a certain proportion of equity through the company's own funds to achieve the synergy effect between the two companies in the product sales end. According to the company's unified arrangement, I led a team to conduct on-site due diligence on the wealth management company to be invested. During the due diligence process, I had a comprehensive interview with Mr. Lu and the company's management, and visited the wealth management stores located in the high-end community in Shanghai. Overall, the development strategy of this wealth management company was relatively aggressive. And through comparative analysis with authoritative external data, it was found that the competition in the wealth management market in China's first- and second-tier cities was relatively fierce and sufficient. Therefore, the risk assessment report issued by the risk management team concluded that "it is not recommended to invest". After a comprehensive discussion by the company's management, the investment was finally abandoned. Afterwards, Mr. Liu sent an email to the risk management team, clearly stating in the email that the independent, objective, and fair risk assessment and suggestions issued by the risk management team were very important, and he hoped that the independence and objectivity would be maintained in the future.

2.3 Enhancing the Value of Risk Management Reporting

Verbal work is a very important task for the risk management team. Risk management reports are the carriers of this work, the crystallization of the team's wisdom and labor, and also the bridge and link for communication between the risk management team and senior management. Given that risk management is a specialized job, in financial institutions, apart from the Chief Risk Officer and the risk management team, few people systematically learn risk management knowledge, and even fewer people take professional risk management exams such as FRM (Financial Risk Manager) or PRM (Professional Risk Manager). Most senior executives may only have a conceptual and systemic grasp of risk management and pay less attention to specific details. Moreover, due to the busy schedules of senior executives, they rarely have time to read each risk management report thoroughly. In a nutshell, while ensuring professionalism, the risk management team needs to enhance the readability and conciseness of the report. The reader should be able to understand and grasp the content of the report in the shortest possible time, and such a report will be valuable. Generally speaking, risk management reports can be divided into regular periodic reports and irregular special reports.

2.3.1 Regular Periodic Reports

Regular periodic reports generally include risk review reports for individual projects or products, and monthly, quarterly, and annual risk management reports at the company level. The content and format of regular reports are relatively fixed. According to my personal experience, a report also follows the "Pareto Principle" (i.e., the "80-20 rule"). The truly valuable part of the report often accounts for only 20% or even less. Therefore, such reports can fully adopt the PPT mindset, with as concise text as possible, and appropriate use of graphics and tables to highlight key points and core content. For example, when I worked in a trust company, I tried to take the monthly risk management report as a breakthrough to improve the efficiency of risk management work. The main approach was to make significant adjustments to the original monthly report format and content, both reducing and appropriately adding. On the one hand, the original nearly 20-page length was greatly compressed, mainly presented in the form of charts and tables to improve the reading efficiency of the company's management. On the other hand, specific suggestions for risk management were added to allow the company's management to fully pay attention to the thinking of the risk management team.

2.3.2 Irregular Special Reports

Irregular risk management special reports are diverse, ranging from research and analysis of a market or industry to in-depth analysis of a product or company. Such reports need to have a certain depth and breadth, and they are often a great opportunity to showcase the style of the risk management team. Therefore, these reports must follow the path of high-quality goods and polish each report into a fine piece with a craftsman's spirit.

Here is an example. In July of the year I worked in the securities company, the credit risk in the Chinese bond market showed an upward trend, and dozens of bonds were downgraded in external credit ratings. Against this background, in July of that year, I took the initiative to organize and write a special report titled "Analysis and Suggestions on Credit Risk of Proprietary Bond Business." In the report, I conducted a one-by-one analysis and study of all bonds held in the company's proprietary position except for government bonds and financial bonds. In the report, I also fully sorted out the bonds with higher credit risk and proposed targeted risk mitigation measures. The timeliness and professionalism of this report were highly affirmed by the company's management. More importantly, since then, the company's management has started to truly pay attention to and value the credit risk of bonds, and has held several special meetings on credit risk management. As far as I know, as of 2023, there has never been a default in this company's nearly 100 billion yuan scale of proprietary bonds, and even the downgrade of external credit ratings is very rare.

2.4 The Ultimate Strategy of Retreat in Extreme Situations

The "Thirty-Six Stratagems" (also known as "Thirty-Six Tactics") is a military book summarized according to the outstanding military thinking and rich combat experience of ancient China. The "36th Stratagem of Retreat" mentioned in the book refers to the act of fleeing when the situation is extremely unfavorable in war. In risk management work, there are times when the company's management, especially the top leader, does not understand or even misinterprets the work of risk management. At the same time, the company's management makes many unreasonable demands and unrealistic ideas for risk management, and it is impossible to change in the foreseeable future. In such extreme situations, risk management practitioners need to boldly use the 36th stratagem, "A wise bird chooses a good tree, and a wise minister chooses a good master." Below are two real-life workplace examples.

2.4.1 The First Case

A risk manager, Mr. Yan, once told me a true story. Many years ago, Mr. Yan worked in a trust company in China and encountered a change in the company's management personnel. The new general manager of the company, Mr. Zhang, was very autocratic and often put a lot of unreasonable pressure on the risk management team in order to quickly increase the scale of the company's managed assets. Once at a company management meeting, Mr. Zhang openly said to the company's Chief Risk Officer, Mr. Tong: "If our company does not approve a trust loan project that has been approved by other trust companies, I will give you a yellow card. If our company does not approve a trust loan project that has been approved by other trust companies and the project does not default in the end, I will give you a red card." Obviously, in such a company, the risk management team was put in a situation where they were at the mercy of others. Faced with such a general manager, the Chief Risk Officer and almost the entire risk management team chose to resign collectively. Although it was a helpless choice, it was also a manifestation of emotional intelligence.

2.4.2 The Second Case

One day in the second half of 2018, I happened to meet the head of the risk management team of a private equity fund company, Mr. Fan, at a forum. Mr. Fan told me that the company was recently discussing granting the chairman a special right - a "single vote approval right" for investment projects. "Single vote approval right" means that even if the company's investment decision committee votes down a proposed investment project, as long as the chairman approves in the end, the project can still be approved. I have often heard about the general manager or chairman of a company having a "single vote veto right" for projects, but the "single vote approval right" is quite new. Mr.

Fan had already decided to leave the fund company at that time because he had truly felt that the company had almost become a one-man show for the chairman. Risk management has become a decoration within this company, losing its meaning and value of existence, "If the skin doesn't exist, where will the hair attach?"

3. Emotional Intelligence In Interacting With Business Teams

It is often seen that some risk practitioners in financial institutions complain on social media that the relationship between the risk management team and the business team is like a married couple, often having small quarrels every three days and big quarrels every five days, which not only delays work but also spoils the mood. At the same time, many financial institutions in China use a 360-degree assessment method, in which all teams, including the business team, grade the risk management team at the end of the year. According to my personal observation and survey, the scores of the risk management team are often the lowest among all the middle and back-end teams. Darwin's theory of evolution pointed out that "it is not the strongest of the species that survives, nor the most intelligent, but the one most responsive to change." The risk management team needs not only to adapt to getting along with the business team but also to live in harmony, which requires emotional intelligence. The famous Hong Kong entrepreneur Li Ka-shing once said, "Solve problems with emotional intelligence, face problems with emotional intelligence." The following discussion on the topic of emotional intelligence in the interaction between the risk management team and the business team will be divided into three aspects.

3.1 Upholding the Bottom Line

Risk management work is the most in need of a bottom line

and is also the most in need of upholding the bottom line. The bottom line of risk management work must absolutely not be a "Maginot Line," which can be easily bypassed by the business team. I personally believe that the bottom line in risk management work mainly includes three aspects: first, the bottom line of professional ethics; second, the bottom line of professional judgment; and third, the bottom line of work quality.

3.1.1 Upholding the Bottom Line of Professional Ethics

Since risk management cannot directly generate revenue, the compensation of the risk management team is usually at the average level in the financial institution, neither too high nor too low. The compensation of the risk management team absolutely cannot be compared with the compensation of the outstanding business team. If there is such a thought that hopes to obtain a high income through risk management work, it would be a dangerous signal. Professional ethics are a high-voltage line, and no member of the risk management team should touch it. Professional ethics are also the North Star, pointing the way for the harmonious coexistence of the risk management team and the business team.

For example, when the risk management team travels on a business trip with the business team, it is permissible for the business team to pay for ordinary work meals, and it would be even better if it could be on an AA basis. However, high-specification banquets should not be attended, nor should gifts from the business team be accepted. "He who eats others' food is short of speech, and he who takes others' hands is short of strength." Mr. Zhang, the head of the risk management team of a financial holding group, once shared his experience with me. Since Mr. Zhang has been working in foreign financial institutions for a long time, he has formed such a principle of handling affairs: "The individual and the risk management team will not accept invitations to dine from subordinate enterprises and business teams, and will always design reasonable excuses to decline in advance." Mr. Zhang's approach is worth learning from.

3.1.2 Upholding the Bottom Line of Professional Judgment

The financial industry is an industry that operates risks, and the business team is risk-seeking. The idea of hoping that the business team can "grasp both business and risk control, and both hands must be strong" is a good initial intention, but the reality often becomes the business team focusing on business while neglecting risk, or even ignoring risk. Therefore, the risk management team must maintain prudence and objectivity in its work, make rigorous and professional judgments, and its voice must be substantial and authoritative, so as to convince others with reason and establish prestige.

Let's take a real example. From 2012 to 2016, the mobile internet industry in China developed rapidly. In early 2016, a business team of the trust company I was in found a Shenzhen-based IDC (Internet Data Center) company. The company was established for only one year, with a registered capital of only 10 million yuan, and it was unknown in the industry, but the overall valuation of the company exceeded 1 billion yuan. The business team designed a limited partnership structure to invest in this IDC company. In the transaction structure, a large private group from Zhejiang could act as the junior party and guarantee the minimum return of the preferred funds. Within the trust company, the business team repeatedly emphasized that this project could be regarded as a credit financing project, not an equity investment project. However, after internal discussion and review, the risk management team believed that this project could not be classified as credit, and should be reviewed according to the standards of equity investment. In addition, the risk assessment report also pointed out that the valuation of the invested company was obviously too high, and it was not recommended to invest. The committee members at the company's investment decision meeting also fully recognized the professional judgment of the risk management team, and the project was eventually rejected.

3.1.3 Upholding the Bottom Line of Work Quality

Risk management is a job with high professional requirements. Every member of the risk management team must firmly uphold the bottom line of work quality and must not relax the requirements of quality because of some urgent needs of the business team, otherwise it would satisfy others but hurt oneself. Sometimes it is not only unable to satisfy others but also hurts oneself, leading to a lose-lose situation.

Let's take an example. In April 2018, the financial holding group I was in approved a project plan submitted by a business team to invest in a private placement of shares of a Chinese A-share listed car company. However, due to external reasons, the private placement of shares of this car company was delayed. In late August of that year, the private placement of shares of the car company was finally approved by the China Securities Regulatory Commission and was about to be issued. In order to compete for more private placement shares, the business team submitted another project plan to invest in the private placement of shares of the car company and urgently requested the risk management team to complete the review and issue a risk assessment report within one day. The reason given by the business team was that the group had reviewed it in April. In response to this, the risk management team rejected the unreasonable requirements of the business team and gave two reasons. The first reason is that the materials submitted by the business team in April were based on the financial data of the target company in 2017, but by August 2018, the company's semi-annual report for 2018 had been released. The company's fundamentals have changed, and the risk management team needs to analyze seriously. The second reason is that the risk manager who participated in the review in April has been transferred, and the new risk manager needs to familiarize and understand the project. Finally, while ensuring the quality of work, the risk management team worked overtime to complete the risk assessment report, but it was not completed within one day. In this way, it not only upheld the bottom line of work quality but also met the urgent requirements of the business team as much as possible, and ultimately achieved a win-win situation.

3.2 Learning to Respect

In the first five years after graduating from graduate school, I was engaged in front-line credit business in commercial banks. This work experience told me that the business team should be given full respect. There are two main reasons: First, the business team directly creates revenue and profit, supporting the daily operation of the middle and back-end teams, including the risk management team. Second, the demand for new risk management positions also comes from the prosperity of financial institution business. Only financial institutions with continuous growth in income and profits may expand the size of the risk management team. To truly respect the business team, each member of the risk management team must internalize and externalize it. The risk management team can only win the respect of the business team by truly understanding and learning to respect the business team. This can be done from the following three aspects.

3.2.1 Cherish the Labor Achievements of the Business Team

In China, finance is the core of the national economy. The financial profession is a respectable and prestigious profession in the eyes of the general public. In the financial workplace, there is a common "floor effect", that is, the financial industry gathers a large number of excellent talents, and those who are not excellent have been excluded from the financial industry. At present, in the business teams of excellent domestic financial institutions, most employees have a master's degree or above, and many also have an educational background from overseas prestigious schools. After studying for many years and spending a lot of money from their families to obtain degrees, when working in the financial workplace, they always hope that their labor achievements can be respected by others.

For the business team, an important labor achievement is the project or product declaration form, due diligence report and other written materials. A report usually has more than 30 pages (font size 5, single spacing), and the report for a complex project or product is even longer. These materials are usually the crystallization of the business team's overtime work and hard work. Therefore, the risk management team not only needs to carefully study the reports and materials submitted by the business team, but also needs to fully understand the content and logic of the report. When encountering doubts and confusion, communicate and exchange with the business team in a timely manner. For high-quality reports, do not be stingy with praise. In this way, the business team can truly feel that their efforts have not been in vain, and their labor achievements have at least been valued and affirmed by the risk management team.

3.2.2 Show Care, Concern, and Affection

Due to the Sword of Damocles of performance assessment indicators hanging overhead, the work pressure on the business team is often beyond the imagination of ordinary people. I have had similar work experiences, so I deeply understand and empathize with this. After I engaged in risk management work, I would visit the business team's office area in my spare time to connect emotionally. During lunch breaks, I often dined with the business team. During the meal, I would inquire about the progress of business development, the problems and difficulties encountered in the process, and sometimes offer my own thoughts and suggestions.

I personally believe that doing so has two major benefits: on one hand, it allows for a full understanding of the dynamics of the company's business operations and to grasp the progress of projects or product advancement, preparing in advance for risk management work and being proactive. On the other hand, it gives the business team a feeling of being cared for, loved, and looked after. After all, the risk management team deals with various different products and projects every day and has a clear understanding of external regulatory requirements and management's risk preferences. The risk management team can provide guidance to the business team in terms of business direction and project selection, helping the business team to take fewer detours and waste less time, achieving performance indicators "more, faster, better, and more economical."

Although risk management is cold, the hearts of the members of the risk management team are warm and passionate. After engaging in risk management work, I have suggested many times that the members of the risk management team change their previous work style. The risk management team should not wait for the business team to come to them but should take the initiative, look for opportunities, and enhance communication and mutual trust.

3.2.3 Promote the Touching Stories of the Business Team

In my more than ten years of career, I have dealt with more than 100 business teams. Overall, I feel that most business personnel are very dedicated, have a high sense of responsibility and commitment to their work. There are many stories that not only moved me deeply but also continuously inspired, encouraged, and even urged me. I often share some typical deeds of the business team and promote them within the company.

In 2015, I encountered such a touching incident. In July of that year, a post-90s graduate, Mr. Luo, who had just joined the company and was engaged in front-line trust business, went to Qinghai Province, China, to expand the business. Qinghai Province is located in a high-altitude area, with an average altitude of over 4000 meters. Mr. Luo encountered altitude sickness. Coupled with overwork and unadapted diet, he had a high fever of 40 degrees Celsius on the second day of arriving in Qinghai and was taken to the local hospital by his colleagues for treatment. However, Mr. Luo still did not forget his job responsibilities, preparing various application materials and due diligence reports for the project while hanging saline solution. He insisted on completing the due diligence work with a sick body and ultimately successfully completed the project. For this story, I have suggested that the company's management promote it among the majority of employees.

3.3 Think from the Perspective of Others

In the workplace, "thinking from the perspective of others" is probably one of the most frequently mentioned terms. For the risk management team, thinking from the perspective of others means thinking about the needs and appeals of the business team from their point of view, considering the company's business development in a practical way, and also reflecting this kind of thinking through specific actions.

3.3.1 Time-Limited Service

The British historian C. Northcote Parkinson proposed the famous "Parkinson's Law" in 1958. This law pointed out sharply that "in an organization, personnel will continue to increase like a pyramid, everyone is very busy, but the efficiency of the organization is getting lower and lower." Therefore, in order to break the curse of Parkinson's Law, the risk management team needs to incorporate time management into their work, to be urgent about the business's urgency, and to think about what the business thinks. For example, when I worked in a financial holding group from 2017 to 2019, the group management required the risk management team to issue risk assessment reports within a time limit of five working days, and this timeliness of the work was included in the performance assessment. My personal requirement is even stricter, for routine and standardized businesses and projects, the report should be issued within 2 days, and for more complex and innovative projects, it should not exceed 4 days.

In addition, in order to complete the performance, the business team often works "5+2 (five working days and two weekends), day and night (regardless of day and night)." The risk management team also needs to take the initiative to adapt. When I worked in the financial holding group, in order to speed up the progress of the project, it was a common occurrence for the risk management team to travel on weekends for due diligence or to write risk assessment reports, and even working overtime on statutory holidays was also a common state. For example, in March 2018, there was a sudden surge in project declarations in the group. At that time, due to the tight manpower of the risk management team, the whole team worked overtime during the Qingming Festival. During the three-day holiday of Qingming Festival, the average daily sleep time of each person was less than 4 hours, and finally, the review work of all projects was completed. Each business team in the group was deeply touched by this and had even more respect for the risk management team.

3.3.2 Active Participation

Before 2019, financial innovation in China was rapidly changing, and the integration of finance and the real economy was continuously deepening. The types of innovative products and emerging industries that financial institutions participated in were also increasing. For these relatively unfamiliar new products and emerging industries, the risk management team needs to break the original "fight when the enemy comes, block when the water comes" work model. The risk management team needs to take the initiative and use creative thinking to get involved in advance and participate with the legal team and other third-party intermediaries, laying the foundation for subsequent risk management work. This approach just confirms the first habit in Stephen Covey's "The 7 Habits of Highly Effective People" - "Be Proactive."

Here is an example. In May 2015, a business team of the trust company I was in discussed cooperation on asset securitization business with a large foreign-funded financing leasing company. The business team had a preliminary communication with me about this potential business. At that time, I keenly realized that similar new businesses would become a new growth point for the company. I not only actively participated in external asset securitization training but also consciously strengthened related business learning and increased communication with the business team. In June of that year, when the business team officially declared this project, the risk management team was well prepared. Both the business team and the company's management fully affirmed the initiative and professionalism of the risk management team. The asset securitization business of the financing leasing company also became the main business direction of this business team.

3.3.3 Active Promotion

One of the important responsibilities of the risk management team is to formulate various risk management systems, business risk management guidelines, and other programmatic documents, which will provide direction and guidance for future business development. Therefore, these documents are closely related to the interests of the business team. Of course, these documents will fully solicit the opinions of the business team during the drafting process, and most financial institutions in China probably do the same.

However, after the risk management documents are issued

within the financial institution, it is common for the business team to organize self-study, and only when there are problems or doubts will they ask the risk management team. Such an approach is often passive, and the learning effect may not be as expected. In order to do things well, the ideal approach is to organize an internal training session for the whole company within a few working days after the risk management documents are issued. The risk management team needs to make the corresponding PPT documents, preach the key points in the documents to the business team, and answer questions on the spot during the training session, which will be more effective.

3.3.4 Personnel selection

"Put oneself in others' shoes" is a working concept, but it is not easy to form such a concept overnight. In risk management work, to effectively practice "put oneself in others' shoes", the members of the risk management team need to have the experience and background of working in the front office as much as possible. Therefore, when forming the risk management team and recruiting risk managers externally, attention should be paid to whether the candidates have the work experience in the front office. My personal observation and the experience of my peers have proved that risk managers with more than 2 years of working experience in the front office will be more handy in risk management work.

Of course, such ideal candidates are not everywhere in China, but are particularly scarce, even hard to find. Therefore, for risk managers who lack the work experience in the front office, they can be arranged to go to the business team for a period of rotation. During the rotation period, risk managers can truly participate in various business works, and truly experience and feel the hardships and pressures of the business team. When they return to the risk management position, they will naturally understand the true meaning of "put oneself in others' shoes".

When I worked in the trust company and the financial holding group, the company had similar arrangements and received very good expected results.

4. Emotional Intelligence In Collaborating With Team Members

In 2017, I had a brief stint working with a risk manager, Mr. Xu. In my impression, Mr. Xu was highly competent, diligent, and sincere. However, in the year-end performance assessment, Mr. Xu unexpectedly ranked at the bottom of the entire risk management team. Later, I learned that some team members felt Mr. Xu lacked team spirit. Risk management is not a one-man show but a grand chorus of a team. It requires concerted effort rather than individual action. This section will discuss "emotional intelligence in collaboration with risk management team members" and will cover three different types of members: newcomers, senior staff, and team leaders.

4.1 Newcomers to the Risk Management Team

Newcomers to the risk management team include college graduates and those who have switched careers to risk management, such as transferring from the business line to the risk control line. Newcomers are the fresh blood and the main force of the risk management team. At the beginning, each newcomer is inevitably full of passion, with unlimited expectations for work, and hopes to make achievements quickly and stand out. This mindset is understandable. As an old Chinese saying goes, "One must eat one bite at a time and walk one step at a time." Risk management work requires time for accumulation, experience, and professional tempering. At the same time, newcomers need to rely on the team for survival and development. Therefore, newcomers need to do the following three things well.

4.1.1 Be Eager to Learn

Henry Ford, the founder of Ford Motor Company, once said, "Whether you are 20 or 80, if you stop learning, it means you are old." For newcomers, it is even more important to take the initiative to learn and be good at learning. Learning should not only be targeted but also pay attention to methods and skills. In addition to mastering the relevant theories, technologies, and tools of risk management, it is also necessary to work hard in the following two aspects.

First, master the external regulatory requirements and internal system requirements. Some people may wonder, "The external regulatory requirements should be mastered by compliance personnel, which has little to do with risk management!" This idea is very wrong. Regulatory requirements themselves have included the most basic elements of risk management. At the same time, these regulations and systems need to be not only studied but also memorized and understood thoroughly, and need to be reviewed regularly so that there is confidence in work. Just imagine, when the team leader or other members of the risk management team consult some issues, newcomers can answer freely and accurately, and give specific sources. Surely the whole team will look at this newcomer with new eyes! At the beginning of 2010, when I switched to a securities company and was responsible for the risk management work of bond proprietary investment business, I was a newcomer to the company's risk management team. Due to the lack of similar work experience, I sorted out all the regulations issued by domestic regulatory authorities on bond business and compiled them into a manual. I also spent several days memorizing the important content and usually took out this manual for review. I felt much more at ease during work.

Second, keep track of and learn about new products and

industries quickly. There is a famous Moore's Law in the field of computers. During the period of vigorous financial innovation in China from 2012 to 2019, Moore's Law began to take effect in the financial industry. Newcomers should maintain sensitivity, freshness, and curiosity about new products, new businesses, and emerging industries. In 2015, I went to a trust company to engage in risk management work and became a newcomer in the trust industry. It was the time of innovation and transformation in the trust industry, with new businesses such as consumer trust, land trust, public welfare trust, asset securitization, and factoring being continuously introduced. At the same time, the fields in which trust companies participated were expanding from traditional real estate and government financing platforms to emerging industries such as drones, IDC (Internet Data Centers), digital copyrights, shared travel, and online dramas. In response to this, I not only widely searched and collected various materials for learning but also often discussed and shared my thoughts with members of the company's risk management team. In addition, I also took the initiative to suggest that the company invite external experts to conduct targeted special training for employees.

4.1.2 Learn to Ask Questions

Work is like doing scholarship; one must learn and ask questions. However, for newcomers, not every problem requires asking, nor should everything be questioned. Asking questions is an art, and it is important to learn how to ask effectively.

Firstly, consider how to ask before posing a question. The purpose of asking is to get an answer that solves the problem. However, the responses to the same question can vary when asked to different people. The way a question is asked can also elicit different answers. Therefore, newcomers in the risk management team should not only think about what to ask but also consider who to ask for the most comprehensive and professional response. Additionally, newcomers should consider how to express their questions concisely and plainly.

Secondly, the same question should only be asked once. For newcomers, encountering various issues at work is quite common, such as questions about work processes. Newcomers should take notes of colleagues' answers and commit them to memory. Remember, the same question should only be asked once. Repeatedly asking the same question can leave a negative impression, with team members potentially viewing the newcomer as careless or unfocused. Repeated inquiries can also be seen as a disrespect for the responder's effort. Once a negative impression of a newcomer is formed within the team, colleagues may be less willing to answer their questions.

Thirdly, do not ask questions that should not be asked. Risk management work involves access to sensitive information, including insider information and trade secrets. Newcomers should refrain from asking about such matters, adhering to the principle of not inquiring into what should not be known. In financial institutions, the backgrounds of risk management team members are diverse, with varying values and personalities. Some newcomers may be curious about their teammates and inadvertently inquire about personal privacy. In modern society, privacy is highly valued. Therefore, newcomers should avoid initiating such questions in their interactions with team members. As the saying goes, "Trouble comes from talking too much," an inappropriate question can sometimes harm the cooperation and friendship among team members.

4.1.3 Work Smartly

Work requires learning by doing and doing while learning, which applies to risk management work as well. However, many people often simplify risk management work as mere hard work, thinking that being like a hardworking and patient old ox is sufficient. In fact, this is not the case; risk management work also requires smart work to achieve more with less effort, which is especially crucial for newcomers.

One is to prioritize work. Each risk management position has several job responsibilities, and some positions even have more than ten. Work must have priorities, otherwise, grasping everything will lead to poor results. My personal work idea is to "do the most urgent things and the most important things". Specific which are the most urgent and important things can be communicated and confirmed with the team leader. When I just started working in the securities company in the risk management position, I communicated with the team leader to determine the scope and priority of my work. Specifically, formulating the risk preference for the company's bond investment (such as the access criteria for bonds) and determining the risk tolerance (such as the maximum duration and the highest leverage ratio of the bond investment portfolio) were the most urgent tasks. In addition, the informatization construction of risk management was my most important work.

The second is to be good at taking work notes. "A good memory is not as good as a bad pen." When I worked in the securities company, Mr. Li, the Chief Risk Officer of the company, required everyone to take good notes during the meeting and also arranged for someone to write the meeting minutes. One of my important responsibilities after joining the company was to be responsible for writing the meeting minutes, and I gradually developed the habit of taking work notes. During my four years of working in the securities company, I filled up six notebooks. This professional habit of taking work notes has been retained until now. Of course, there are "three musts" for taking notes: one is to record clearly and completely, the second is to summarize, generalize, and refine in time, and the third is to review frequently. In addition, I was surprised to find that taking work notes is a "kill two birds with one stone" thing, and there are four benefits. The first is to improve the ability of shorthand and quick note-taking. The second is to exercise the ability of language organization and induction. The third is to help understand the ideas and thoughts of others, especially the leaders. The fourth is to facilitate the implementation in the future work.

4.2 Senior Staff Of The Risk Management Team

John Maynard Keynes, the founder of modern macroeconomics, once said: "Economists should be like dentists, humble and competent." This sentence also applies to senior staff of the risk management team. Senior staff usually no less than 30 years old, embodying the saying "thirty is the age to stand firm." These staff members not only possess a wealth of experience in risk management but are also capable of handling responsibilities independently. They play a pivotal role, acting as the backbone and the ballast stone of the team. To enhance the cohesion and collaborative spirit of the entire risk management team, senior staff must excel in three key areas.

4.2.1 Be Supportive

Senior staff often take on the role of mentors and career guides for newcomers, facilitating their rapid growth. Some may worry, "Won't this create direct competition, affecting the future promotion and even survival of senior staff?" Such concerns are unnecessary and reflect a petty mindset. Only by enabling newcomers to take on responsibilities quickly can senior staff free themselves from their original tasks. This allows senior staff the opportunity to engage in new and more challenging management roles, thereby realizing their full potential and value. Otherwise, they may forever remain just a cog in the machine, stuck in the same place. Mentoring newcomers can be approached from the following two aspects.

Firstly, guide them through daily work with hands-on training. For instance, in the risk review of equity investment projects, senior staff can categorize past projects and select the most representative and typical ones for newcomers to study. They should provide necessary explanations and timely answers to questions. Senior staff should also encourage newcomers to participate independently in project reviews, ensuring strict adherence to processes, quality, and professional standards. When appropriate, guide newcomers to organize and summarize the workflow, risk control points, and report elements into an operational manual, making it replicable and scalable for future reference.

Secondly, remind newcomers of the red lines in their work. For example, in securities companies and fund management companies, an important and routine task in risk management is real-time, dynamic monitoring of investments. The trading and holding situations of securities such as stocks and bonds in each investment account are fully visible. If a risk manager misuses this information with ill intent, the consequences can be very serious and dreadful.

When I worked in securities and trust companies, there were strict and mature mechanisms for experienced staff to guide newcomers within the company. After joining the financial holding group, I submitted a written proposal to the group's management about implementing a mentorship mechanism within the group. The mentorship mechanism is also an effective way to prevent operational risks.

4.2.2 Think Diligently

In their work, senior staff must keep their eyes on the ground and look up at the sky. They need to frequently think about their work and the future of the team from the perspective of the team leader or even the company's management. This lays the foundation for taking on more important management responsibilities in the future.

In March 2018, I attended a talent development workshop held by the financial holding group. At the meeting, the group's

Chief Risk Officer, Ms. Shi, said, "In work, talents should do one, look at two, and think about three." I personally think Ms. Shi's words make a lot of sense. Senior staff in the risk management team should not just see themselves as operational hands; they cannot focus only on their own small area of responsibility. They need to "eat what's in the bowl, look at what's in the pot, and think about what's in the vat." Only by doing so can one's future career path become wider and wider.

For senior staff, in their own work, they need to imagine themselves as team leaders, using a "magnifying glass" to examine their work and determine which aspects need improvement and enhancement. At the same time, they need to stand at the height of the entire company or even the industry, using a "telescope" to overview their work and consider which areas need innovation and breakthroughs.

For comprehensive affairs and tasks of the team or the company, such as office process optimization, work efficiency improvement, incentive mechanism improvement, etc., senior staff should try their best to make suggestions, offer their rational thinking, and provide solutions. When they become team leaders or take on more important management responsibilities in the future, they will inevitably face and deal with these difficult issues. It's better to plan ahead now rather than being caught off guard at that time.

4.2.3 Be Humble

In the 1990s, there was a popular TV drama in China called "The Dynasties". There is a very influential line in this TV drama - "Striving is not striving, not striving is striving," which is very suitable for the financial workplace. In the workplace, many people often attach great importance to external things such as year-end evaluations, promotions, and salary increases, and they often argue fiercely for these. I personally think that senior staff in the team need to have a spirit of humility and not actively compete for these. After all, the financial workplace is a talent market with full competition. Those who can become team leaders of risk management or senior managers of financial institutions have gone through layers of selection and survival of the fittest. We need to believe that the leaders' eyes are bright, their hearts are like mirrors, and their IQ and EQ are high enough. As long as employees are passionate about their work and responsible for their careers, what belongs to them will eventually be theirs, and no one can take it away. Similarly, what is not yours will not be yours in the end, and you can't take it by force.

When I was working in risk management at the securities company, there was a senior risk manager, Ms. Qian, in the risk management team. Ms. Qian's work was outstanding, and she was very modest. Every time the team was preparing to recommend her for the company's outstanding employee, Ms. Qian gracefully gave the opportunity to other members of the team. There is an old Chinese saying, "Gold will always shine." When the company established an asset management subsidiary, considering Ms. Qian's solid professional foundation and rich work experience, she was chosen to be the head of the risk control team of the subsidiary. After 2020, Ms. Qian has become the general manager of a medium-sized asset management company in China.

4.3 The Leader of the Risk Management Team

"The train runs fast, all depends on the locomotive to lead." "A bear soldier is a bear, a general is a bear for a group." These catchy Chinese sayings fully illustrate the importance and key role of a team leader. In 2015, I applied for the position of General Manager of the Risk Management Department of a joint venture public fund. During the interview, the company's CEO, Ms. Liu, asked me, "As the leader of the risk management team, what do you think are the three most important things in your work?" After pondering for a moment, I replied, "Choose the right person, listen more, hold fewer meetings."

4.3.1 Choose the Right People

The team leader is responsible for grasping the overall direction and doing top-level design. As for how to do specific things, it can be authorized to capable people. If the team leader is involved in every detail, they often end up picking up sesame seeds while losing watermelons.

Everyone's ability and work preference are different. Some people are good at writing, some are good at organizing and coordinating, and some are strong in communication. Therefore, for the team leader, the first thing is to arrange the right person to do the right job, which is very important. My personal experience and workplace observation have proven that once the wrong person is chosen, not only can the work not be carried out smoothly, but it can also affect the morale and fighting spirit of the whole team.

Choosing the right person can not only promote the smooth progress of work but also produce "herd effect" and "leverage effect." Specifically, the team can continuously attract excellent and suitable talents to join. At the same time, more and more challenges and difficulties will be overcome, and the team's performance will continue to improve.

In the process of selecting people, one should not only look at the length of work experience in related work but also not just at education, major, and professional certificates. People with strong execution and a deep understanding of risk management should be chosen. I personally prefer those who majored in non-economic fields (preferably science and engineering majors) in undergraduate studies and chose finance in graduate studies. Because in practice, I find that such people are very logical, organized, and methodical, which is very compatible with and matches the risk management work.

4.3.2 Listen more

In 2015, an article titled "Why Harvard is First-Class - Observations and Thoughts from a Half-Year Visit" was widely circulated in China. The first reason mentioned at the beginning of the article is "the air of freedom and tolerance", and this kind of air also needs to be introduced into risk management work. Because risk management itself is a challenging job with no standard answer. At the same time, risk management practitioners are full of wisdom and have their own minds. There is an old Chinese saying: "Three humble shoemakers can outwit Zhuge Liang." The head of the risk management team needs to embrace the spirit of tolerance and equality, and strive to play the role of a listener.

Firstly, listen more to the members' thoughts on the work. General George Patton, a famous World War II general in the United States, once said: "If everyone thinks the same, then someone is not thinking." In practice, the people who know the risks best are often the risk managers working on the front line, not the head of the risk management team. At the same time, risk management itself is dynamic, and the team leader should encourage every member to speak freely. Encourage everyone to express their professional thinking and professional judgments honestly, so that the team members can have a sense of existence and belonging. The team leader should affirm, listen to, and follow the good advice for the correct opinions, so that the team members can have a sense of achievement and satisfaction. Otherwise, risk management work is likely to become like seeing only a part of the picture or like a blind man touching an elephant.

Secondly, listen more to the team members' career aspirations. In the financial workplace, apart from the boss, everyone is a worker or, to use a more polite term, a "professional manager." Every member of the risk management team will have expectations, thoughts, and plans for their future career. For example, some members may wish to dedicate their lives to the risk management profession. Others may see risk management as a stepping stone to future front-line business positions or to move to more back-end support roles. These aspirations are reasonable and understandable. The team leader should listen to the members' thoughts on their careers when necessary and provide advice and assistance as much as possible. This will demonstrate the team leader's care for the personal interests of each team member, and perhaps the future leaders in risk management will come from this team.

4.3.3 Learn to Conduct Meetings

If you were to ask a financial professional, "What is the most important thing in your work?" Most would likely reflexively answer, "Meetings." Meetings are a double-edged sword; they can be very beneficial when used correctly but can be quite detrimental when misused. There is an important law in economics called "the law of diminishing marginal returns." When there are too many meetings, their marginal benefits can be very low or even negative. Of course, having fewer meetings does not mean not having any; meetings are necessary but should be conducted with the following principles in mind for the risk management team.

Firstly, hold important meetings. For example, the weekly (or monthly) risk management team meetings are essential as they allow the team leader to accurately and comprehensively grasp the work status of the entire team. Additionally, meetings to discuss significant projects and important work mobilizations are indispensable. However, these important meetings should not be mere formalities; they must be conducted thoroughly and result in the substantial resolution of issues or specific work arrangements. Any other meetings should be minimized.

Secondly, conduct well-prepared meetings. Just as one

does not go to war without preparation, one should not hold meetings without preparation. Before each meeting, key elements such as the agenda, objectives, and expected duration should be communicated to participants in written form, such as via email, and it should be clear whether speaking is required. Moreover, the meeting facilitator must be well-prepared in advance. My personal habit is to rehearse the relevant speech content and meeting process the night before each meeting.

Thirdly, strive to hold short meetings. Generally, the team leader acts as the moderator in risk management team meetings. Therefore, the team leader must control the progress of the entire meeting like a conductor at a concert, focusing on important content and key information without digressing. Everyone's time is valuable, and wasting others' time is akin to theft. Regular and routine meetings should be completed within half an hour, and the moderator can place a watch on the table as a reminder to keep the meeting concise.

After completing the initial draft of the article, I sent it to Ms. Shi via email, as mentioned at the beginning of the article. After reading it, she replied to my email, saying, "The catchphrase I use at work—'Risk management is a strong physique plus a flexible posture'—has been expanded into an article by you, and it makes sense; I will definitely keep this article well!"

RISK MANAGEMENT PROFESSIONALS' WISDOM, TRUSTWORTHINESS, BENEVOLENCE, COURAGE, AND STRICTNESS

During the Chinese traditional Lunar New Year in January 2020, I found myself with some idle time at home and casually picked up "The Art of War" by Sun Tzu from my bookshelf for reading. I had read "The Art of War" once in junior high school purely out of interest in military affairs. At that time, I understood it vaguely. More than twenty years have passed, and my insights from rereading it are profoundly different. The book mentions that "a general should possess wisdom, trustworthiness, benevolence, courage, and strictness," a standard that is also very suitable for risk management professionals. Currently, China's risk management talent is evolving from a phase that focused on quantitative expansion in previous years to a new stage that emphasizes quality improvement. The quality of risk management professionals can be evaluated and measured through these five qualities: wisdom, trustworthiness, benevolence, courage, and strictness, all of which I believe are equally important and indispensable. This article will discuss this topic.

1. The Wisdom Of Risk Management Professionals

"Wisdom" has many explanations in the "Xinhua Dictionary," such as IQ, intelligence, and wisdom. American psychologist Raymond Cattell divides a person's intelligence into two major categories: fluid intelligence and crystallized intelligence. Fluid intelligence represents a person's potential intelligence, which is greatly influenced by genetic factors and peaks around the age of twenty, then begins to decline. In contrast, crystallized intelligence refers to the intelligence obtained through mastering socio-cultural experiences, closely related to continuous learning and the accumulation of various experiences. I personally believe that for risk managers, "wisdom" should refer more to crystallized intelligence, which should at least include three aspects: "knowledge system," "management art," and "forward-looking thinking."

1.1 Construction of the Knowledge System

Investment master Warren Buffett has a well-known theory of the moat. Specifically, a truly great company must have a moat that can last for a long time, thereby protecting the company to enjoy a high return on invested capital. This moat theory actually has a wide applicability. For example, in the risk management workplace, the knowledge system is the toolbox of the risk manager and also the moat around the castle of the workplace. The broader this moat is constructed, the more obvious the comparative advantage in the competition of the risk management workplace will be. According to my personal experience and observation, risk management work will have different focuses in different types of financial institutions, and the knowledge system of risk managers should "change according to need."

For example, in transaction-driven financial institutions such as securities companies, fund companies, and futures companies, risk management tends to focus on the measurement and monitoring of risk. The work content of risk management will focus more on quantitative modeling, risk pricing, and dynamic monitoring. The knowledge system of risk management professionals needs to include professional knowledge such as mathematics, statistics, computer science, and finance. In project-driven financial institutions such as commercial banks and trust companies, most members of the risk management team are responsible for analyzing counterparties, due diligence, and risk review. Therefore, the corresponding knowledge system needs to be mainly based on professional knowledge such as finance, accounting, auditing, and finance.

At the same time, the knowledge system is closely related to the position of the risk manager. As the individual's position continues to improve, the content carried by the knowledge system will increase exponentially. For example, the knowledge system of the head of the risk management team, in addition to covering the knowledge system of other employees in the department, also needs to integrate more knowledge of team collaboration, performance incentives, human resource management, and other non-risk management knowledge. The knowledge system of the Chief Risk Officer, in addition to having the knowledge system of the head of the risk management department, needs to further increase macro-level knowledge such as corporate strategy, corporate culture, and institutional diplomacy, as well as other explicit disciplinary knowledge such as philosophy and Chinese studies.

The risk management techniques, tools, and methods I mentioned above are, at best, part of the existing body of knowledge. However, the ever-changing changes in the real economy and the financial industry have given birth to an incremental environment. Risk management professionals need to adapt to this incremental environment, and simply applying and integrating existing knowledge is far from enough. Only through continuous learning, especially acquiring new incremental knowledge, can they build a risk management knowledge system that is suitable for an incremental environment.

1.2 Cultivation of Management Artistry

During my tenure in a securities firm specializing in risk management, our team leader, Mr. Wang, often emphasized that excellence in risk management requires a transformation from a technical professional to a composite management talent. Although one's intelligence quotient might be innate and not change significantly over time, management artistry is not something one is born with; it is something that must be acquired and continuously refined through experience.

1.2.1 Reading Management Books and Putting Them into Practice

When I was working in a trust company, the general manager, Mr. Liu, suggested that employees read management books. In China, there is an overwhelming and varied selection of management literature, so discerning and selective reading is essential. I personally favor the works of management guru Peter Drucker and also read excellent articles published in the "Harvard Business Review." In addition, among the vast array of ancient Chinese literature, there are many works rich in management thought, such as the "Four Books" and "Five Classics." Chinese historical records document the story of "Zhao Pu, the founding prime minister of the Northern Song Dynasty, governing the world with half of the 'Analects of Confucius'." Therefore, in my spare time, I also choose to read selected chapters from these books.

"Read ten thousand books, travel ten thousand miles." Beyond reading, management artistry must be mastered through practice. Of course, the practice of management is embedded in the everyday details of work. For example, taking the lead in drafting a risk management document, organizing a special risk management inspection, initiating a risk management meeting, and so on, are all opportunities to hone management skills.

1.2.2 Learning from Those Around You

"In the company of three, there must be one who can be my teacher!" This saying is particularly applicable in management. In practice, risk managers can learn the art of management from the following three groups of people.

Firstly, learn management artistry from leaders. In my view, those who are promoted to be the heads of risk management teams, Chief Risk Officers, general managers, and chairmen in financial institutions must have their unique and valuable approaches to management that are worth learning. We should pay more attention to the management style and methods of leaders, engage more in discussions with leaders about the principles and techniques of management, and of course, learn to critically assimilate and absorb these lessons.

Secondly, learn management artistry from colleagues. An excellent financial institution often gathers elites from all over, each bringing their distinctive management artistry. Working with outstanding colleagues on valuable and interesting tasks is a kind of happiness. At the end of 2017, the financial holding group where I worked recruited a colleague, Ms. Shen, who had long worked in a top global consulting firm. Through collaboration with Ms. Shen, I mastered the skill of using concise and infectious PowerPoint presentations to demonstrate work ideas and results. At the same time, I also had colleagues who chose to pursue an MBA. By communicating with these colleagues, I could indirectly learn management concepts and methods from MBA courses.

Thirdly, learn management artistry from peers. Many methods and skills in risk management work have strong common characteristics. During my time working in risk management at securities firms, trust companies, and financial holding groups, I regularly participated in risk management experience exchanges with peers. In addition, I took the lead in establishing the Risk Management Alumni Club of Shanghai University of Finance and Economics in November 2017. An important function of this club is to rely on the strong alumni network of Shanghai University of Finance and Economics to regularly hold risk management peer exchange activities between financial institutions. The club aims to become a shared platform for financial risk management that connects various financial institutions, financial institutions with regulatory bodies, and the practical field with academia.

1.2.3 Learning from Your Past Self

I always believe that your past self is the best teacher for an individual. In today's fast-paced work, although it is difficult for risk managers to "reflect on oneself three times a day," it is still necessary to regularly summarize one's own experiences and lessons, especially the lessons learned. "One cannot step into the same river twice." For an excellent risk manager, it is not appropriate to make the same mistake twice or to fall in the same place twice.

However, sometimes it is strange that some shortcomings of a person will reappear in the management work, which can be described statistically as "autocorrelation." But in the workplace of risk management, if some shortcomings of work reappear repeatedly, they may very well end one's career. I have heard of some cases and seen some with my own eyes. Therefore, when one discovers or is reminded of shortcomings in work, it is necessary to pay high attention. Analyze the reasons in time, solve them seriously, and if necessary, record them and remind oneself at all times. The "Harvard Business Review" has conducted research and found that one of the four major elements affecting happiness is the "ability to learn from mistakes." This ability is not only a talisman for career survival but also a key to open the door to promotion.

1.3 Cultivating Forward-Thinking

I usually enjoy watching football matches. In a 2016 World Cup match in Germany, the commentator during the live broadcast said, "A great midfielder on the football field is one who can pass the ball to the position where the forward can run, not just to where the forward is standing." I think this is the forward-looking thinking of an excellent midfielder. In layman's terms, forward-looking thinking is "foresight." There is a large state-owned investment group in China with the slogan "Foresight Achieves the Future." Investment requires foresight. Similarly, risk management also requires foresight, "Foresight Achieves Risk Management." Here are two examples.

1.3.1 The First Example

At the beginning of 2010, I left a foreign bank and chose to engage in risk management work at a securities firm. At that time, I was thinking about the development of China's capital market in the next ten years, and one of the conclusions of my thinking was that the domestic financial derivative product market would have a great development and prosperity. For this reason, on the one hand, I actively prepared for the Chartered Financial Analyst (CFA) exam and usually paid attention to research reports and news reports in the field of derivative products. On the other hand, starting from September 2012, when I used my spare time to pursue a doctoral degree, I chose derivatives as the research direction for my doctorate, and my doctoral thesis naturally selected derivatives as the topic. Between 2010 and 2013, the securities firm where I was located successively carried out risk management systems for financial derivative products such as stock index futures, interest rate swaps, Treasury futures, and options. I represented the risk management team in participating in the design of these product risk management systems, and the related work was also affirmed by the company's management.

1.3.2 The Second Example

In the first half of 2013, a vice chairman of the China Securities Regulatory Commission was preparing to visit the securities firm where I was to research risk management work. In order to prepare for the corresponding reporting work, the entire risk management department was mobilized and worked overtime. I can't remember how many times the report and presentation documents for the report were revised. Finally, after the company's chairman, Mr. Pan, reviewed all the reporting materials, he personally sent an email. In addition to expressing condolences for the hard work of the risk management team in the email, he also proposed a high-level view that the company's future risk management work needs to strengthen proactivity and foresight.

As a risk management professional, in addition to doing my personal daily work well, I also look forward to the future of the industry in which the company is located for the next 5-10 years. Based on this, I predict the development of the company in the next 5-10 years. Finally, I plan my personal risk management work for the next 5-10 years. Only in this way can we truly serve the long-term interests of shareholders, the sustainable development of the company, and the personal career development.

2. The Integrity Of Risk Management Professionals

In Shanghai, China, there is a time-honored accounting firm called "Lixin Accounting Firm" and a school specializing in training financial and accounting talents, "Shanghai Lixin University of Accounting and Finance" (formerly known as "Shanghai Lixin Accounting College"). The founder of this accounting firm and school is Mr. Pan Xulun, a renowned accounting master in modern Chinese history in the 1920s and 1930s. Mr. Pan is also one of the financial figures I admire most in modern Chinese history. It is by following Mr. Pan's culture of "establishing credibility, valuing credibility, and keeping credibility" that this firm and school have been able to stand firm to this day.

On Wall Street, there is a saying: "Short wins are not as good as long wins, and long wins are not as good as eternal wins." I personally believe that the secret to eternal victory in risk management is "integrity." "With integrity, one stands; without integrity, one falls." The term "integrity" in the "Xinhua Dictionary" is explained as one of the meanings "honest, not deceiving." In this memorandum, I would like to expand on the meaning of "integrity," which specifically includes three elements: "honesty, trustworthiness, and self-confidence."

2.1 Upholding the Bottom Line of Honesty

On May 13, 2017, an article titled "What Else Should We Learn from Buffett Besides Investing" was published in the "Securities Times" of Chinese media. The core idea of the article is the need to learn from Buffett's honest and realistic character. For example, at the Berkshire Hathaway shareholders' meeting held on May 7, 2017, Buffett and Munger openly admitted that they had overestimated IBM's stock and had made a wrong judgment on Google and Amazon stocks and did not buy them. Although Buffett also emphasized that tech stocks such as Microsoft, Google, and Facebook have become his favorites, he frankly said that he actually did not understand these companies. I think it is precisely Buffett's honest character that has maintained Berkshire Hathaway's supreme position in the investment field.

Let me give another example from my personal experience. After graduating from graduate school in 2005, I started working at a Shanghai branch of a joint-stock commercial bank. According to the unified arrangement of the branch's human resources department, graduates needed to rotate through the counter of the sub-branch's business department first. Every day after the business department's business hours ended, the last routine process was to check the consistency of the cash amount and the accounting amount in the computer system, that is, to check whether the accounts and reality were consistent. Only when these two amounts are completely consistent can employees go home. Occasionally, there would be a situation where the cash amount and the accounting amount differ by a penny or a few cents. To find this seemingly small difference, it often took several hours. At that time, I thought that the employees could just make up the difference themselves, so why bother to go through such a big trouble! In response to this, the person in charge of the business department repeatedly emphasized the requirement of honesty in work, and the difference must be reported truthfully, and employees are strictly prohibited from making up the difference privately. Although it has been more than ten years, and I have long left the bank, the requirement of honesty in work has always constrained and influenced me.

Based on years of work experience and lessons learned, I believe that "honesty" is the most basic moral requirement for risk management work. The reason and logic behind this are self-evident. Risk management needs to follow the principle of objectivity, which means that people engaged in risk management work need to carry out their work from an objective and neutral standpoint. The premise of objectivity is honesty. Only honesty can ensure the authenticity of the information provided by the risk management team, the objectivity of risk exposure, and the fairness of duty performance. Only honesty can make the decision-making of the management based on information reasonable and reliable. Otherwise, there will be a "small error leads to a big mistake," which will ultimately damage the interests of shareholders and the overall interests of the company, and of course, personal interests will also be affected.

For risk managers, honesty in work is mainly reflected in the following two aspects:

Firstly, when reporting, it must be truthful and nothing can be concealed, nor can there be selective reporting. For example, when I was engaged in risk management work in a financial holding group, the group often held project approval decision-making meetings. I not only required each member of the risk management team to report the risks of the project comprehensively and truthfully to the decision-making committee during the meeting, but I also took the lead in practicing this requirement.

Secondly, "know what you know, and do not pretend to know what you do not know." The innovation of China's financial industry is rapidly changing, and risk management professionals will often encounter new businesses and new products. Even the best risk managers cannot understand all businesses and products all the time. Therefore, for situations that are really not understood, not clear, and not familiar, do not cover up or hide. At the same time, it is necessary to break the bottom of the pot and ask until it is completely clear and understood.

Once, when communicating with colleagues from the group's human resources department who were responsible for recruitment, I made a request. Specifically, before the company issues the appointment notice, a comprehensive and detailed background check must be conducted on the candidates for risk management positions. If it is found that the personal resume of the candidate does not match the real situation, no matter how excellent the candidate is, they will not be hired.

Only by establishing a risk management team within a financial institution that adheres to the moral bottom line of honesty can the business team be at ease, the company's senior management can be relieved, and the external regulatory authorities can be reassured.

2.2 Building a Culture of Trustworthiness

It is often said that "the market economy is a credit economy." The financial industry is also an industry that abides by credit. Risk management work is a job based on credit. According to my career experience and personal observation, in a financial institution, in addition to the management, the members of the risk management team should be the most eye-catching and respected. Therefore, in addition to the honesty mentioned above, the risk management team also needs to create a culture of trustworthiness, "Once a risk control officer speaks, it is as good as done."

"Gold cups and silver cups are not as good as the praise of others." Where does the reputation and praise of risk management professionals come from? It comes from the "words must be done, actions must be fruitful" in daily and bit-by-bit work. Only in this way can the risk management team win the trust and trust of the front-line business team, other middle and back-end departments, and the management. People often say "uphold righteousness and be extraordinary," I want to say in the field of risk management is "uphold trust and be extraordinary."

I personally think that trustworthiness includes two levels, the first level is "keeping one's word," and the second level is "achieving results."

2.2.1 Keeping One's Word

Let's take a real case as an example. A trust company in China promoted Mr. Shen to be the assistant to the general manager of the risk management department in 2018. Mr. Shen was in charge of the risk management work of real estate business. Once, the business team had an urgent real estate project and hoped that the risk management department could arrange the on-site due diligence of the project as soon as possible. Mr. Shen promised to arrange it within a week. But later, for some reason, it was not implemented. The business team reflected this situation to the company's president. As a result, Mr. Shen was removed from his position as assistant to the general manager of the risk management department of the trust company in less than two months. The lesson of "breaking trust" is profound!

Generally speaking, risk management work that is written on paper and has a clear time node is usually highly valued and promoted according to plan. This is because there are inquiries from the company's management, regular internal audits of the company, and other third-party explicit constraints. However, the work promised verbally, due to the lack of explicit constraints, may be somewhat distant from the requirement of "words must be done." For example, in risk management work, you will hear members of the risk management team communicate with colleagues from the business department and say, "I'll take a look at the materials first, and I'll reply to you before work is over," but in most cases, there is no news. This kind of unintentional "broken trust" behavior needs to be alerted. We can use an Excel table to make a "Today to do list," and check it before work is over to see if today's work is completed today.

2.2.2 Achieving Results

Some people simply understand keeping promises as keeping one's word, which is not wrong. But in my opinion, this is at most 50% correct, and the remaining at least 50% should be "achieving results", otherwise it is a kind of mediocrity at work. Of course, achieving fruitful actions is by no means a perfunctory or hasty conclusion, nor is it starting strong and ending weakly; it requires full commitment, even 120% effort. At the same time, how to verify whether you have fully committed, I think a feasible way is to ask your true and pure self. If the answer is "yes," it means you have done it. If the answer is "no," unfortunately, there is still some distance to go. What the specific reasons are requires self-analysis.

I have always had the idea of establishing a "credit file" for employees within financial institutions during work, and to include it in the annual individual performance assessment. Reward those who keep their word, and punish those who break it. With the development of big data and artificial intelligence, the mechanism of personal work credit files is technically feasible at present. Only when such a mechanism is truly established can we avoid the "bad money driving out good money" phenomenon in the workplace. Tolerance of the untrustworthy is the greatest injustice to those who keep their word.

2.3 Persist in the Path of Self-Confidence

I usually like to communicate with some peers who are engaged in risk management work. Some peers are a bit confused, confused, and even lack confidence in the future of the risk management profession; especially in August 2018, I met a Mr. Fang who was engaged in risk management work in a large commercial bank. Mr. Fang has been engaged in risk management work for about half a year and is eager to understand the future of the risk management profession.

There is a very popular SWOT analysis method in management studies, where S stands for strengths, W for weaknesses, O for opportunities, and T for threats. As a more senior person in the field of risk management, I am full of confidence in the future of the risk management profession. This is because the risk management profession is full of opportunities and potential, which is the O in SWOT that is prominent, for the following three reasons:

2.3.1 Overall Macro Situation

With the continuous advancement of China's interest rate marketization reform, the continuous improvement of the RMB exchange rate formation mechanism, coupled with the domestic economy moving from a stage of high-speed growth to a stage of high-quality development, the various risks faced by financial institutions in China are increasingly emerging. Financial institutions are increasingly paying attention to risk management and increasing their investment in people, finance, and materials for risk management. However, compared with foreign mature financial institutions, China's financial institutions' risk management is still in its infancy. In the future, as China's financial market moves towards developed financial markets, the requirements for risk management are bound to benchmark international advanced levels.

2.3.2 External Regulatory Requirements

Due to the nature of my work, I pay more attention to various external regulatory regulations and requirements in the financial industry. In 2016 alone, the China Securities Regulatory Commission and the China Securities Association issued five regulatory regulations for risk management in the securities industry, including the "Securities Company Risk Control Index Management Measures" and the "Securities Company Comprehensive Risk Management Standards." In September of the same year, the China Banking Regulatory Commission issued the "Comprehensive Risk Management Guidelines for Banking Financial Institutions" for the first time. These regulatory regulations reflect the Chinese government's high attention to the risk management of financial institutions, thus pointing out a broad avenue for the risk management profession to some extent.

2.3.3 Prospects for Derivative Product Market

One of the essences of finance is risk management, but risk management requires tools and means, among which the most important risk management tool is the derivative product. In August 2022, the "People's Republic of China Futures Law" was officially implemented. However, at present in China, both the on-site derivative products (futures and options of the exchange) and the off-site derivative products (such as forwards, swaps, off-site options, etc.) are still in the primary stage of market development. Compared with mature financial markets, there is a significant gap in the scale, breadth, and depth of China's derivative markets. However, Chinese financial institutions are full of confidence in the future development of the derivative product market.

With the development of derivative products, on the one hand, risk management will expand from mere management through systems and processes to risk quantification and modeling management. On the other hand, it also poses new requirements for the risk management of derivative products themselves. Accordingly, the demand for technical and measurement aspects in risk management will increase significantly, providing a broad space for development and a stage for financial engineering talents to display their talents.

Moreover, I have always had an idea and wish: to establish a "Risk Management Day" globally, to make this day a holiday for risk management professionals around the world, thereby truly improving the whole society's awareness of risk management work and the importance given to risk management professionals.

3. The Benevolence Of Risk Management Professionals

In the Chinese "I Ching," there are two famous sayings that are still widely circulated today: "Heaven's movement is ever vigorous; the superior man should constantly strive to strengthen himself. Earth's condition is receptive devotion; the superior man should carry virtue." The core of "great virtue" is "benevolence." Therefore, since ancient times, the Chinese have paid great attention to and valued "benevolence," such as benevolent governance, benevolence and righteousness, benevolent love, and other words that highlight this characteristic and tradition. In the eyes of many, "benevolence" is a kind of cultivation, a kind of self-restraint, a noble and perfect character. In risk management work, benevolence is a way of working, a way of treating people, and a way of handling affairs. So, let's talk about the "benevolence" of risk managers in this section.

3.1 Learn to Discover the Bright Spots of Others

Let's start with a small story. A calligrapher dipped his brush in ink and dotted a large piece of white paper, then showed this calligraphy work to friends and family, asking them what they saw. The answer was the same: "It's just a black dot." This made the calligrapher feel a bit helpless because no one mentioned the 99% of the paper that was white. This story just confirms that in work, it is much easier to find fault with others and look for other people's problems than to discover other people's strengths and perceive other people's progress.

Risk management work is done by people, more precisely, it relies on a team. Therefore, each member of the team needs to learn to discover the bright spots of others. A person's bright spot includes the following two meanings.

First is the individual's strengths and advantages. "Everyone has strengths and weaknesses." In a risk management team, everyone has their strengths and advantages. For example, some people are good at financial analysis, some are proficient in quantitative modeling, some are strong in logical thinking, some are good at communication and coordination, some are diligent in writing expression, some pay attention to detail, and so on. Therefore, an excellent risk management team should be the optimal configuration of each member's strengths and advantages, so as to achieve the efficiency and effectiveness of risk management.

The second is the individual's trajectory of progress. Rome was not built in a day, and the Great Wall was not built in a day. Risk management work has its natural laws and cannot engage in blind leaps forward. Only by pooling everyone's progress in work can the optimization and improvement of the overall work be ultimately achieved.

So, how can we effectively discover the bright spots of others? Based on my personal work experience, there are the following two suggestions for reference.

First, let employees sort out and summarize for themselves. We can let each employee of the risk management team write down and speak out their strengths and advantages, and under the premise of seeking truth from facts, exhaust all possibilities. In addition, in the monthly, quarterly, and annual work summaries of the employees, encourage them to write about their progress during this period and the aspects of the work they are satisfied with.

Second, the team leader must be attentive. The team leader must learn to be good at discovering and timely recording the bright spots of each team member, and publicize them at the right occasion and the right time. Here, I think of the person who was the head of the risk management team when I was working in the securities company, Mr. Wang. Mr. Wang would remember the strengths and advantages of each team member with his heart, and discover everyone's progress in work with his heart. Praise at the department work meeting and other occasions, so as to play an exemplary role and exert the power of the model.

By continuously discovering the bright spots of others, it can increase a sense of closeness, trust, and tacit understanding among team members, and continuously push forward the risk management work.

3.2 Learn to Be Tolerant of Others

Since I came to Shanghai University of Finance and Economics to study for a graduate degree in September 2002, I have been working in Shanghai after graduation, and in the blink of an eye, I have lived in Shanghai for more than twenty years. I deeply feel the inclusive spirit of "all rivers run into the sea" that this city has, which is also one of the reasons why I love Shanghai and am willing to regard Shanghai as my second hometown. In the past few years of working in the field of risk management, I have deeply felt the importance and value of being tolerant of others. The tolerance here can specifically include the following two aspects.

First, we should be tolerant of different opinions in risk management work, and even critical opinions. Risk management is not a natural science, but a social science, an art. And the existence of risk management as an independent discipline has only a development history of only sixty years. There is no absolute authority in the field of risk management, and there is no absolute truth. Therefore, in the process of risk management work, we cannot have a single voice, and the evolution of risk management is itself an inclusive development process.

Second, we should be tolerant of non-subjective mistakes in

the risk management work of others, and not criticize in a one-size-fits-all manner. According to my personal observation, the reasons for the emergence of mistakes in risk management work come from two aspects. One is the subjective mistakes, such as the mistakes caused by the professionals' lack of diligence. Obviously, this kind of mistake can be completely avoided, and once it occurs, it must be criticized or even punished. The second is the objective mistakes, which can be controlled but cannot be avoided. Unless you don't do it, objective mistakes will inevitably occur. There is an old Chinese saying, "No one is perfect," which refers to objective mistakes. Risk management itself is a very challenging job. Work often involves some unfamiliar areas, some unknown worlds. Risk management work is extremely challenging to a person's IQ, EQ, and professional knowledge. The objective deviations and mistakes in risk management work are considered normal, and the team leader and other members should be tolerant.

In addition, risk management team leaders and Chief Risk Officers and other risk management leaders need to "fully understand employees and fully understand employees" in their work. Learn to admit the imperfections in work and accept the differences among employees. I remember when I was working in the securities company, the Chief Risk Officer Mr. Li once talked to me. In the communication, Mr. Li sincerely told me that he wanted to hear what I thought were his shortcomings in his work. I said bluntly, "Mr. Li, your biggest shortcoming is that you are an idealist and a perfectionist. You hope that every risk manager can be as good as you!" After hearing this, Mr. Li thought for a while and replied, "It's very pertinent."

3.3 Learn to Be Grateful to Others

I personally like to read the "Meditations" written by the ancient Roman philosopher-emperor Marcus Aurelius. At the beginning of this work, Marcus Aurelius is grateful to his ancestors, parents, teachers, close friends, and others for learning character, knowledge, skills, and other foundations of life and governance from them. Generally speaking, we would be grateful to those who help us, support us, and those who are in the same trench with us. However, we also need to be grateful to another kind of person. Who exactly are they? Let me tell a story first.

There was a prince in ancient India who was very happy after winning a great battle with his troops. At the celebration, the prince thanked those who raised him, wise generals, brave soldiers, and meticulous attendants in turn. However, the prince's father (the emperor) believed that the prince had overlooked a very important person to be grateful for. The prince was puzzled. Finally, the emperor said that they should also be grateful to their enemies, because it was the enemies who ultimately achieved this victory.

In the workplace, of course, there are no enemies, but there are those who find faults with your work, look for shortcomings in your work, and seek deficiencies in your work. In my opinion, these people are like catfish, and risk management work should welcome these catfish and be grateful for the catfish effect they bring. Without the existence of these catfish, the entire risk management work may seem peaceful on the surface, but it also loses the motivation and source of progress and improvement.

"There is no love without reason, and no hate without reason." In risk management work, there will often be no groundless criticism or unfounded accusations. At the beginning of 2010, I jumped from a foreign bank to a securities firm to engage in risk management work. The Chief Risk Officer, Mr. Li, was very strict with work and pursued perfection. As a newcomer to risk management, I was often the most criticized during every risk management meeting. The reasons for my criticism included many aspects such as professional level, work ideas, and ways of doing things. But now, looking back, I find that it was precisely during that time that I made the fastest progress and grew the most. To this day, I am still grateful for the "catfish effect" that Mr. Li brought to my personal risk management work.

3.4 Learn to Treat Superiors and Subordinates Equally

Many people compare the workplace to a place of fame and fortune, so they often carry a strong utilitarian and opportunistic color in the workplace. For example, being respectful or even flattering to superiors, but being arrogant or domineering towards subordinates. Such employees are probably often encountered in the workplace, but such employees are probably not respected by anyone. An excellent risk management professional should treat subordinates and superiors the same way because not only are superiors one's workplace resources, but subordinates are also one's workplace capital, for the following three reasons:

Firstly, risk management work is definitely not a solo performance by one person, but a collective performance by an orchestra. From the perspective of team cooperation, only with the full cooperation and unity of subordinates can risk management work be smoothly advanced, and it is possible to maximize the expected target value.

Secondly, in a financial institution, superiors do have the right to nominate employees for promotion but not the final decision-making power. The final decision-making power is often in the hands of the management. Before exercising the final decision-making power, the management will fully consult the opinions of the majority of employees, especially the employees of the department and team (i.e., "public opinion"). In my more than ten years of work in finance, there have been countless examples of superiors' nominations being vetoed by public opinion.

Lastly, in the process of job-hopping, potential employers will not only pay attention to the candidates' reporting objects (i.e., superiors) but also pay attention to the number of candidates' managed teams, team composition, and other subordinate situations. Sometimes they even find out about some subordinates through various channels to understand the candidates from the side.

In 2016, I applied for a position as the head of the risk management department of a newly established financial institution. At that time, the risk management department of this financial institution had not yet been established. During the interview, the deputy general manager in charge of human resources at the financial institution said: "If you take on this position in the future, I hope you can bring some excellent colleagues from the existing risk management team to join, because if you are a truly outstanding leader, your colleagues will sooner or later follow you." This statement deeply touched me, and I think only a truly "benevolent" risk management leader can have a group of followers and form a long-term stable and like-minded alliance of risk managers.

4. The Courage Of Risk Management Professionals

In 2019, many friends of mine who were engaged in risk management work chose to transform their careers. Specifically, they adjusted from risk management positions to other positions, including front-line business positions and back-end financial management positions. I was very curious about their reasons for leaving the risk management position, and the answers I received were various. But after summarizing and generalizing these answers, I concluded that the core reason was the lack of a "courageous" character. So, let's talk about the "courage" of risk management professionals.

4.1 Have the Courage to Bear Pressure

I often communicate with friends in the financial industry who are engaged in risk management work, and we all feel that the pressure of risk management work is great. I remember a friend once said jokingly, "If you like someone, let him (her) engage in risk management; if you hate someone, also let him (her) engage in risk management." When I heard this sentence, everyone laughed. But after laughing, after pondering this sentence, it is quite reasonable.

I think the pressure of risk management work has two levels: the first level is normal work pressure. Like other professional work including finance, investment, and auditing, risk management, as a profession, requires a sense of responsibility and a sense of commitment, which naturally leads to professional pressure. The second level is based on the particularity of risk management, making this job have an "extraordinary pressure." This kind of pressure comes from the company's management and business team. Let's mainly talk about the second level of pressure.

First, let's look at the management. Some executives have such a view: "Since the financial institution has hired the risk management team at a high salary, there should be no risk. If there is a risk, such as overdue debt projects, because these projects have been on-site due diligence by the risk management team in advance, and have been reviewed, and the risk management team did not object at that time, the risk management team should bear the responsibility for such risky projects and be held accountable." I am resolutely opposed to such views. Both at the company's internal work meetings and at external risk management forums, I, on behalf of the risk management team, solemnly stated the corresponding position and attitude. Risk management has its inherent flaws and insufficiencies. Risk management does not equal the elimination of risk. Risk management is to ensure that the risk undertaken by the company is within a reasonable and tolerable range. This tolerance is definitely not a "zero tolerance" for risk. For risky projects, as long as the risk management team has maintained due diligence, due diligence, and professionalism in the project's due diligence, review, and post-investment management process, it should be exempted from responsibility. In addition, in response to the management's unrealistic requirements for risk management, the risk management team must have the courage to manage expectations of the management and resolutely correct the cognitive bias of the management.

Next, let's look at the business team. In terms of risk management, the business team's requirements for the following two aspects are almost impossible to meet: one is risk control efficiency, always wanting it to be as fast as possible; the second is risk control standards, always wanting it to be as loose as possible. Therefore, the business team and the risk management team are often in a state of game. When the business team fails to meet the performance targets, when doing attribution analysis, some reasons will be projected onto the risk management team. The business team will think that the company's risk control requirements are too strict, or the work efficiency is too low, etc., which makes the business lack competitiveness in the market, leading to difficulties in business development. I participated in a risk management training organized by Shanghai Advanced Institute of Finance in 2012. In the training, a senior risk management professional shared a true story that happened in the Royal Bank of Canada. The bank's trader attributed his poor performance directly to the back-office risk management personnel. The trader believed that the bank's risk control restricted his performance. As a result, the trader directly sent an email to the bank's top leaders to complain about the risk management department, and demanded the bank to immediately dismiss the relevant risk managers with a very tough tone.

4.2 Have the Courage to Face Challenges

The financial industry in China is generally a red ocean, although there are still some niche areas that remain blue oceans. Therefore, to survive and develop, Chinese financial institutions inevitably need to undergo business transformation and even strategic adjustments. Risk management will inevitably be adjusted accordingly, and to some extent, it needs to be planned in advance and planned ahead. In such a financial ecosystem, risk management professionals will inevitably face unprecedented challenges. Let's take two cases as examples.

4.2.1 The First Case

In early 2015, I joined a trust company to engage in risk management work. At that time, the company's management had keenly seen that the growth space for traditional municipal and real estate trust businesses was not large, and they were seeking new business breakthroughs. At that time, the state was vigorously supporting the photovoltaic industry, which had also become a venture investment industry. The management needed to discuss whether to enter this industry. Of course, the photovoltaic industry was absolutely a new field for the company's management and risk management team. After many internal discussions within the management, no consensus was reached. Against this background, the risk management team took the initiative to face difficulties and accept challenges. The risk management team not only studied the various policy documents of the central and local governments on the photovoltaic industry item by item but also studied a large number of in-depth research reports on the photovoltaic industry. In addition, the risk management team also visited several senior researchers in the photovoltaic industry. Finally, they proposed a set of detailed, comprehensive, and feasible risk control plans and measures for the photovoltaic industry's investment and financing business. It was based on the risk management plan and measures that the company's management finally decided to participate in the photovoltaic industry. Subsequently, the investment and financing business in the photovoltaic industry gradually became an important source of operating income and profit growth for the company.

4.2.2 The Second Case

In 2018, a financial institution in China was preparing to enter the inclusive finance business. After extensive demonstration, it was found that the financing business for used cars was still a blue ocean, and it was decided to enter this field. The risk management team was not familiar with this type of business. To meet the challenge, in addition to recruiting personnel with relevant work experience externally, the risk management team also adopted two countermeasures. First, they actively extended their working hours, changing the original "nine-to-five" working hours to "nine-to-nine," thereby leaving more time for collective learning and discussion. Second, they conducted field research on the main used car markets across the country, and in just one month, the members of the risk management team almost ran through the used car markets in the provincial capital cities of the country, communicating face-to-face with a large number of used car dealers and buyers. Finally, the risk management team formulated operable and company-actual risk control policies and plans, laying the foundation for the subsequent business.

For new businesses and new products, on the basis of setting relevant risk management conditions, financial institutions can carry out pilot projects in a "controlled scale, controlled speed" manner. Through pilot projects, it is possible to test whether the preliminary designed risk management plans are effective. Through pilot projects, it is also possible to further refine the key points of risk management and improve the measures for risk control. Through pilot projects, risk management can be more grounded and more effective, thus turning challenges into the driving force for moving forward.

4.3 Have the Courage to Innovate and Break Through

I personally advocate Schumpeter's theory of innovation. I always believe that risk management requires continuous innovation, sometimes even disruptive innovation. Of course, innovation includes institutional innovation, organizational innovation, product innovation, process innovation, and technological innovation. In risk management work, these innovations are all needed and necessary, but I personally prefer technological innovation in risk management. Let's take two examples.

4.3.1 The First Example

In June 2010, shortly after I joined the securities company, a colleague, Ms. Zhang, resigned. Before leaving, Ms. Zhang handed over the risk management work of the margin trading and short selling business to me. In order to apply the knowledge points in the Financial Risk Manager (FRM) exam in daily work, I independently developed a stress testing model for the company's entire margin trading and short selling business. Of course, looking back now, this stress testing model seems relatively simple. The model mainly used the Capital Asset Pricing Model (CAPM). Of course, with the stress testing model, it is possible to measure the safety margin of the financing stocks or short selling stocks from the margin line before the stock market opens every day. This technological innovation was also reported and publicized in the company's internal magazine.

With this successful experience, one of my daily tasks in 2011 was to take the lead in developing a comprehensive risk management information platform for the entire company.

Since there was no ready-made platform solution in the industry at that time, on the one hand, I re-read classic risk management textbooks, and on the other hand, I had multiple brainstorming sessions with the business team and external technology developers. After about half a year of development and testing, the comprehensive risk management information platform was finally completed, and it is in a leading position in the Chinese securities industry in terms of design foresight, function completeness, system practicality, and performance stability.

4.3.2 The Second Example

In July 2017, the State Council of China issued the "New Generation Artificial Intelligence Development Plan." In this plan, it is clearly mentioned to "establish a financial risk intelligent early warning and prevention system." In fact, in the first half of 2017, I was already considering how to integrate technological means with risk management. I also firmly believe that technology has many application scenarios in the field of risk management, which can effectively solve some of the pain points in the current risk management work, thereby greatly improving the efficiency and effectiveness of risk management. Starting from May of that year, I discussed with the IT department and external experts how to combine big data, artificial intelligence, and the full cycle risk management of asset management products. This ultimately improved the digitalization, automation, and intelligence in each link such as project initiation, due diligence, collective decision-making, post-investment management, risk monitoring, and risk disposal. Finally, this intelligent risk control platform was successfully developed and put into daily work. Risk management professionals should become innovators in risk technology, not bystanders.

According to my personal experience, innovation in risk management needs to fully value newcomers, boldly employ newcomers, and leverage their creativity and imagination. Sometimes, even interns can bring innovative inspiration and different ideas to the entire risk management team.

4.4 Have the Courage to Uphold Principles

Let me give an example. In September 2011, due to external factors, the bond proprietary position size of a Chinese financial institution touched the risk limit set at the beginning of the year. This meant that the financial institution would have to sell hundreds of millions of yuan in bonds. It happened to be a stock and bond double kill at that time, and selling these bonds would mean a certain loss. The business team judged that the bond market would bottom out and rebound soon, so they suggested not to sell for the time being, but to sell after the market rebounded. However, since the risk limit was touched, the risk management team firmly demanded to execute the liquidation. In the end, the bonds exceeding the scale limit were all sold, and they happened to be sold at the lowest point of the bond market. About half a month later, the bond market bottomed out and rebounded. At the year-end work summary meeting, the business team naturally mentioned this incident and pointed out that if these bonds that were forced to be sold remained in the proprietary trading account, it would increase the company's profit by tens of millions of yuan. In response, the Chief Risk Officer replied resolutely: "We are engaged in investment business, not speculative trading. The biggest difference between investment and speculation is that investment is principled and disciplined. The risk management team is the last line of defense to guard these principles and disciplines." This sentence illustrates the courage and responsibility of a risk management professional in adhering to principles.

Someone might ask, what are the principles that risk management needs to adhere to? Based on my personal experience and thinking, there are "three benefits" principles.

Specifically, it is beneficial to the overall interests of the company's shareholders, beneficial to the improvement of the company's management, and beneficial to the overall risk control of the company. As long as it is something that conforms to the "three benefits" principle, the risk management team should insist on doing it, promoting it, and have the courage to persist and adhere to it. The persistence in principles must not imitate the Allied Forces of Britain and France who pursued the "appeasement policy" in the early stages of World War II, but should learn from the Soviet Red Army who fought for every inch of land in the Battle of Moscow.

I once heard a fable. If a group of lions is led by a sheep, it can only be called a flock of sheep at best. Conversely, if a group of sheep is led by a lion, it is a pride of lions rather than a flock of sheep! Therefore, a risk management team must be as brave as a pride of lions, and it must be led by a brave leader. Only in this way can the interests and dignity of each member of the risk management team be truly protected, and the value and glory of risk management can be truly defended.

5. The Strictness Of Risk Management Professionals

In July 2019, I had a conversation with several friends engaged in risk management work. During the exchange, Mr. Tan, who served as the Chief Risk Officer at an insurance company, lamented that at the company's executive performance report for the first half of the year, the chairman's evaluation of the company's risk management work was quite low. This left Mr. Tan feeling quite depressed. After much thought, he realized that this situation was greatly related to his usual approach to risk management, which was "too lenient, too loose, and too soft." Based on this, Mr. Tan concluded that risk management must start with the principle of "strictness." Here, we will focus on the "strictness" of risk management workers, discussing two aspects: first, why "strictness" is needed, and second, how to achieve "strictness."

5.1 Why Strictness is Needed

In a nutshell, the survival of financial institutions is inseparable from strict risk management. The financial industry is a brutally competitive jungle, following the law of natural selection. In China's financial industry, there is homogeneity in business, convergence of customers, and uncertainty in the market. Therefore, only those financial institutions that consistently adhere to "strict risk control" can survive.

The innovation and development of the financial industry still cannot be separated from strict risk management. Around 2020, in order to balance the relationship between financial innovation and financial regulation, domestic and foreign financial regulatory authorities proposed the "Regulatory Sandbox." The so-called "Regulatory Sandbox" refers to a "safe space." In this safe space, financial institutions can test their innovative financial products, services, business models, and marketing methods without immediately being subject to regulatory constraints when problems arise in related activities. I have been thinking that the regulatory sandbox is a good idea and an ideal initiative. However, whether the regulatory sandbox can truly be effective and sustainable, in addition to the efforts of the regulatory authorities themselves, largely depends on the endogenous risk management system within financial institutions. Whether this system is effective largely depends on the "strictness" of risk management professionals.

Writing here, I would like to elaborate more on the internal logic of why risk management professionals as individuals need to follow the "strictness" principle. In addition to the reasons mentioned above, I believe there are two important factors.

5.1.1 The Intense Competition in the Financial Workplace

From 2017 to 2019, every working day morning, I would take the Shanghai Metro Line 2 to Lujiazui for work. When getting off at the Lujiazui Station, I distinctly felt the huge flow of people, which should be the largest flow of people in Shanghai during the rush hour. After all, in China, Lujiazui is the area with the highest density of financial institutions and is also the core functional area of the Shanghai International Financial Center. Every time I saw such a continuous stream of people, I couldn't help but sigh that the financial industry is indeed a highland that gathers many excellent talents from both China and abroad. The financial workplace should indeed be the most fiercely competitive workplace.

Based on my long-term observation, among the entire financial workplace, the competition for risk management positions is estimated to be the most intense. Whether it is front-line business personnel or other middle and back-office (such as compliance, finance, products, etc.) employees, they all hope to have the opportunity to join the risk management team. It can be said that in financial institutions, risk management positions are both respected and sought after.

If a person is not strict with themselves in risk management work, slack and muddle along, it is estimated that they will not produce the work performance expected by the management. It is very likely that this employee will be eliminated in the near future. When I entered the trust industry to engage in risk control work at the beginning of 2015, I heard such a story. There is a medium-sized trust company in China that once had a risk management team of 10 people. However, in less than two years, all the original team members were gone. Team members either switched jobs or changed positions. One of the key reasons was that the company's management was dissatisfied with the risk management team.

5.1.2 The Innate Occupational Risks of the Work

When I communicated with some colleagues, I made such a metaphor: engaging in risk management work is like holding a short position in a put option with the company's performance as the underlying asset. I think this metaphor is relatively easy to understand. For example, when a financial institution's business is booming, income is growing rapidly, and profits are high, for members of the risk management team, they can only get a relatively fixed income. Even if the risk management team can get a year-end bonus, the bonus amount is not comparable to the business team and cannot fully enjoy the dividends brought by the high growth of the company's performance. However, on the contrary, when the financial institution's business encounters significant risks or projects have big problems, the risk management team is often directly held accountable, ranging from being criticized to having their salaries reduced, bonuses deducted, or even being dismissed. The occupational risks of risk management professionals are not small.

For risk management professionals, on the one hand, they are managing risks for their employers, and on the other hand, they also need to manage risks for their own careers. Therefore, only by having high standards and strict requirements for themselves can they effectively control their own occupational risks while managing risks for their employers. Finally, a win-win situation of "you win, I win, everyone wins" can be achieved.

5.2 How to Achieve Strictness

In late 2013, I had the honor of attending the Cross-Strait Financial Forum held by the Wang Yanan Institute of Studies at Xiamen University. It was also my first visit to Xiamen. The motto of Xiamen University is "Strive for self-improvement, and stop only at perfection." I think that professionals engaged in risk management should take "stop only at perfection" as their code of conduct. To achieve "stop only at perfection," one must be strict. This strictness can be in two dimensions: one is strict with oneself, and the other is strict with others.

5.2.1 Strictness with Oneself

In 2017, a widely circulated epitaph from Westminster Abbey in London on Chinese social media encapsulated the idea that to change the world, the country, and the family, one must start with oneself. In fact, more than two thousand years ago, the great Chinese thinker Confucius said, "Cultivate oneself, order the family, govern the country, and bring peace to the world." Only by completing self-cultivation can one possibly order the family, govern the country, and bring peace to the world. Therefore, to achieve strictness in risk management, one must start with oneself. If one is to be strict with others, one must first be strict with oneself. I believe that strictness with oneself in risk management can be divided into three levels: strict performance of duties, daring to benchmark, and having a global perspective.

Firstly, strict performance of duties. In September 2018, at the risk management training session for new employees of the group, I mentioned that there are currently two animals favored by the financial industry. One is the black swan, and the other is the gray rhino. The black swan is a metaphor for an event that has a very low probability of occurring but causes a significant negative impact, while the gray rhino represents an event that has a high probability of occurring and causes a significant impact. In the daily work of risk management, our primary responsibility is to accurately identify the gray rhino and to make reasonable suggestions for effectively controlling it. At the same time, we must remain vigilant about the black swan and formulate feasible and comprehensive contingency plans. Therefore, risk management professionals must strictly perform their job responsibilities, handling daily work with a prudent attitude and professional principles. For example, when I worked in the trust company, the due diligence I personally participated in and the risk assessment reports I wrote were all conducted with the strictest requirements and the highest standards. I often advocated to other colleagues that in judicial litigation, the work of the risk management department and the reports issued should exempt the company from liability and also exempt the risk managers from liability.

Secondly, daring to benchmark. In psychology, there is an effect known as the "anchoring effect," which is an important psychological phenomenon. The anchoring effect specifically refers to the phenomenon where people need to estimate a certain event quantitatively and will use some specific values as the starting value, like an anchor that constrains the estimate. Applying the anchoring effect to risk management work, using benchmarking as the anchor will lead to the benchmarking effect. By actively seeking learning objects and then carrying out benchmarking, one can achieve standards, and ultimately complete the evolution and transformation of risk management. I think the benchmarking in risk management can be carried out in two aspects:

Firstly, the benchmarking of the risk control system. Generally, it is to benchmark the financial institutions with the best risk management practices at home and abroad. Of course, in the benchmarking process, it is also necessary to fully combine the institution's own strategic positioning, business situation, team capabilities, and other factors. Suppose a financial institution's business is benchmarked with Goldman Sachs, then risk management must also be benchmarked with Goldman Sachs or even other financial institutions with better risk management than Goldman Sachs. If risk management is benchmarked with Lehman Brothers, it is estimated that this financial institution will not go very smoothly, nor will it go very far.

Secondly, the benchmarking of one's own job. Generally, the benchmarking of one's own job is to look up to the best employees within the company, and sometimes even to the best talents in the industry. Since 2016, Shanghai has held a financial talent selection activity every year, divided into three categories: "overseas financial talent, leading financial talent, and young financial talent." After several rounds of screening, the final talent list is selected and announced. I will carefully read the resumes and performance of these talents, looking for excellent talents that can be benchmarked. If necessary, I will also find the relevant benchmarking talents through various channels and actively seek advice and learn from them.

Thirdly, having a global perspective. China's financial market is becoming more and more open to the outside world, such as the Shanghai-Hong Kong Stock Connect, Shenzhen-Hong Kong Stock Connect, Bond Connect, and the inclusion of A-shares in the MSCI Emerging Markets Index and MSCI ACWI Global Index since June 2018. With the globalization of the economy and finance, financial risks are also becoming global, and the input and spillover of risks will become the new norm. In June 2017, the Lujiazui Forum held in Shanghai had the theme of "Financial Reform and Stable Development in the Global Perspective." In September of the same year, the Financial Street Forum held in Beijing chose the theme of "Financial Reform and Risk Prevention and Control under the Background of Global Economic Change." These two of China's most authoritative and influential financial forums discussed finance in the context of the global market, reflecting to some extent the acceleration of China's financial integration into the global market. Therefore, for risk management practitioners, they must also keep up with the pace of globalization and not limit their horizons and personal thinking to domestic issues, but should have a global vision and a global pattern. It's not just about having an English name to be international and global, but truly needing the concept and cognition to be international and global.

5.2.2 Strictness with Others

I remember in the 1970s in China, there was a popular saying:

"Marxism for others, liberalism for oneself." So, being strict with others is something many people can do, but not necessarily do well, often failing to convince others. I personally believe that being strict with others should follow two "consistencies." Specifically, consistency over time and consistency among individuals.

Firstly, consistency over time. Risk management work unfolds sequentially along the timeline. As a leader of the risk management team, being strict with others in work should have consistency over time. It should not be strict today, lenient tomorrow, and strict again the day after, without significant jumps in strictness. However, we must admit that sometimes our strictness with others can be influenced by personal emotions. For example, during a period when one is in a particularly good mood, the requirements for the team members in work will naturally be more relaxed. On the contrary, during another period when one is upset due to criticism from a leader or other negative factors, one may make excessive demands, pointing out dissatisfaction here and there, and the employees will be exhausted in dealing with it, which is detrimental to everyone. Therefore, leaders need to control their emotions and separate emotions from work, otherwise, it will be harmful to the company's risk management work.

Secondly, consistency among individuals. Risk management work is implemented by a team. For the leader of the risk management team, being strict with each person in work should have consistency among individuals. The leader should not be overly tolerant with employees they value or have a close relationship with, while imposing excessively strict demands on those they dislike or do not value.

Strictness with others often manifests in two aspects: the quantity of work and the quality of work. Sometimes I hear complaints from some risk management peers about the team leader's extra "reliance" on certain employees. Leaders often use the slogan "more work for the capable," assigning as much work as possible to these employees, while the workload of other employees is relatively less, leading to an imbalance in the distribution of workload. Of course, this does not mean that we must adhere to egalitarianism in work. However, if there is a significant difference in the distribution of workload, it will demotivate the morale of employees with less work on one hand, and on the other hand, it may overwhelm the employees with a heavy workload. In addition, in terms of the quality of work requirements, many people believe that employees with high professional levels and strong work capabilities naturally have higher work quality than others. Such a view is also biased. We advocate that everyone should be equal in terms of work quality.

Finally, let me mention that "strictness" must not be for show, not for the sake of being strict, but should be a project that benefits the company and the people. Strictness needs to have a measure and a boundary. Since strictness has a cost, excessive strictness can lead to unnecessary losses in economics, which will bring marginal net losses to risk management work. Any management work, including risk management, is actually pursuing a match and balance between cost and benefit. Outstanding risk management practitioners can find the best match and the optimal balance point appropriately.

ABOUT THE AUTHOR

Wen Si

Wen Si is PhD in Economics, Certified Public Accountant (CPA), Chartered Financial Analyst (CFA), and Financial Risk Manager (FRM). Wen Si has nearly 20 years of experience in the financial industry. He has worked in various institutions, including commercial banks, securities firms, trust companies, and financial holding groups. He serves as a part-time academic supervisor for master's degree students at several universities in China, including Renmin University of China and Shanghai University of Finance and Economics. He has published several works on financial technology, including "Python for Financial Analysis and Risk Management" and "Hands-on Python for Finance".

www.ingramcontent.com/pod-product-compliance
Lightning Source LLC
Chambersburg PA
CBHW071922210526
45479CB00002B/521